This Books Includes a Bundle of Windows 10 and Hacking

Windows 10

The Ultimate Guide for Beginners to Operate Microsoft Windows 10

By Malcolm Schwartz

Table of Contents

Chapter 1: An Introduction to Windows 10

Today, the big players in the computer industry like Google and Apple just give away the operating systems, this has put a damper on how Microsoft has conducted business for as long as we got to know and love the company. For this operating system, Microsoft decided to give it away between the dates of July 29th, 2015 all the way to July, 29th of 2016. Their hopes are that those with a licensed copy of Windows 7 or 8 will upgrade their computer to the newest of operating systems.

The reason behind their bit of change of heart is due to the issues that many have had in the past with having different Windows operating systems. With Windows 10 being the main operating systems as far as Windows goes, it is much easier for app designers to create apps that will work for more people. Before there were many people who had issues because an app may only be used by Windows 8 or 7, now, with the Windows 10 being free for that time period to download and upgrade, there is a larger mass of those that own devices to be able to utilize the applications that are created. Windows 10 is not the standard for Windows based computers.

Some may think that due to the past marketing, Windows will not be able to make money by offering the operating system for free for a year. However, this may seem true by just skimming the surface of their financial plan; digging a little deeper will tell you otherwise. Although they are giving up potential dollars by offering it for free; they are able to design the apps for many, many more people to utilize, and thus recouping their losses on the operating systems. Yes, this benefits the company, but also the users. If you have had past Windows, then you are well aware of the issues that can come up with software only being available for a specific version of Windows. So, everyone benefits.

If you are thinking about the succession of the version of Windows, you might have wondered why there was no Windows 9 released. True be told, there was never a Microsoft Windows 9. They skipped the number 9 and went straight to 10. The reasoning behind this is that the developers and the company believes that this specific operating system deserves more than a 10. In their words, Windows 10 is a "perfect 10".

Minimum Hardware Requirements

Microsoft has always been very great at ensuring that the lower end computers are able to run their system. This is no exception. Windows 10 has much of the same system requirements for Windows 8. If you need to know the specifications of Windows 10, here they are in the simplest of forms:

- **Latest OS**: Ensure that you are running the latest version of Windows - 7, SP1, or 8.1. Make sure that you update to one of those in order to update to Windows 10.
- **Processor**: 1 GB for 32 Bit or 2 GB for 64 Bit
- **RAM**: 1 GB for 32 Bit or 2 GB for 64 Bit
- **Hard Disk Space**: 16 GB for 32 Bit OS and 20 GB for 64 Bit OS
- **Graphics Card**: DirectX 9 or Later with WDDM 1. 0 Driver
- **Display**: 800 X 600

Important Notes About Windows 10

In this section you will learn about some of the special notes that every Windows 10 user should know.

- Those who have Windows 10 Home Edition will automatically get updates through the Windows Update when the updates become available. Windows 20 Enterprise and Pro users will have an ability to postpone the updates. The amount of the time they can be postponed is limited.
- Smaller storage devices like the devices that have 32 GB hard drives or the older devices with a full hard drive may need some additional storage in order to complete the upgrade. You will see instructions that will tell you what you should do while it is upgrading. You need to either insert your USB flash drive or you will need to remove unneeded files for the computer.

- In order to perform an upgrade the computer will need to be connected to the internet. Windows 10 is a bigger file; about 3 gbs.
- To upgrade the device, the factors will go beyond the specifications. This will include the firmware and the driver support, feature support, and the application compatibility. This will be regardless of whether the device meets the system specifications of not for Windows 10.

Logging Into Windows 10

There are three different ways that you are able to log into Windows 10. The three are using a PIN, password, or a picture password. From the login screen, you will be able to switch between the choices of logging into your computer.

In addition to the traditional password logon, Windows 10 has included a picture password and a PIN logon for your safety and the security of the other users. You are able to use Microsoft email accounts to logon or even a local account in order to gain access to your computer. However, there are some conflicts in design that may not allow you to use the picture password or PIN. For example, when you are in Safe Mode, neither of these ways will work and you will have to use the traditional way of logging in using a password. Here are the ways that you can set your login options.

- **Changing Password**: You are able to change your password by going to the Start Menu. Click on the Setting. Select Accounts. Next, you will choose Sign In Option. Hit the button that says Change underneath the Password heading. You will then enter your Current Password. Click on the Next button. You will then be prompted to enter a new password and a hint for your new password. Click on the Finish button.
- **Picture Password**: This will enable you to use a certain picture from the library as your password. You have to use three gestures on the picture that you want to use as the password. For example, you are able to select, draw, and even resize a portion of your picture that you would want. Under the settings application, under the option Picture Password. Click on the Add button. You will type in the user password, and then click OK in order to confirm the account information. Draw three gestures on your picture. Repeat this step and then click on the Finish button in order to exit.
- **PIN**: If you do not want to set up a Picture Password, then you are able to use a PIN in order to log into your computer. Go under Settings and then click on Accounts. Click on the Sin In Options. Select the change button under the PIN section. Enter your password, and then click on the OK button. Next, you will enter a new PIN. Click on Finish.

File Explorer in Windows 10

The File Explorer used to be known as Windows Explorer. It is the way you can get into your computer, whether you are looking for files, settings, or peripherals. This is often where you will begin the search. Windows 10 offers a new look to the interface of the File Explorer, and here is how you can tweak it.

First of all, you are able to customize the Quick access pane that offers important locations, recent files, and recent folders. You will right click on any of the frequent folder to get access to the options. Using your navigation bar that is on the left, you will click and then drag any entry in order to change its order in a queue and to get the most used folders first.

If you do not like Quick access and you would rather start up File Explorer with the old view instead, right click on the Quick access heading on the left side, choose the options, and then select This PC from the menu located at the top.

Chapter 2: How to Uninstall and Reinstall Windows 10 Built In Apps

The applications that are built into Windows 10 are pretty great; however, there are many, many alternatives that are available. You may want to delete one or more apps because you found an alternative that works better for you personally. Do not fret, there is a way that you can uninstall the apps and reinstall them should you want them back.

Uninstalling Windows 10 Built In Applications

Some of the default applications will allow you to manually uninstall them as you would another program or application, while there are others that will need a bit more effort. You will need to use the PowerShell in order to uninstall those that need more effort, as well as for those that you can uninstall in a traditional way.

- To uninstall an app in the traditional way, **right click** on your app and then you will select uninstall.
- For those that you need to use PowerShell for, type PowerShell into your Search Windows box. You must be logged on as the Administrator. Type in **'Get-AppxPackage*AppName* | Remove-AppxPackage'**. Change the

'AppName for your specific application name that you would like to remove.

You might want to check the name of the app before you try to delete it. For example, if you want to delete the weather app, the name is different. It is actually 'bingweather'. So, ensuring that you know the proper name of the app will ensure that you can delete it.

Reinstalling Windows 10 Built In Applications

In order to reinstall your default applications in Windows 10, you will need just one of the command. It will refresh all of your apps and then replace the ones that were removed when you were getting rid of some.

- Type in 'PowerShell' into your Search Windows box and then you will open it as the administrator.
- Type in **'Get-AppxPackage | Foreach {Add-AppxPackage-DisableDevelopmentMode-Register "$($_.InstallLocation)\AppXManifest.xml "'**.
- You will then wait for the process to be completed.

Depending on the computer system, this process can take a bit longer. You may not be able to see the results either until you check the Start Menus and see your applications being returned.

Chapter 3: Fixing Display and Sound Issues in Windows 10

Just like other operating systems, there may be issues that can arise with the sound or the display. In this chapter you are going to learn how to fix the issues that can happen with your own computer using Windows 10. There are bugs that can happen, but is fixable with the information in this chapter.

Fixing Your Sound

In this section you are going to learn the steps that you need to perform in order to fix issues with your sound, or when there is no sound at all.

- You will right click on the sound icon that is located in the taskbar. It is at the bottom of your screen.
- Select the option Playback Devices from your menu.
- Choose your current playback device and then double click on it in order to open the properties.
- Go to the Advance tab and then change the bitrate to 24 bit / 44100 Hz or 24 bit / 192000 Hz, which will depend on the speaker configuration.

After you have done this, check to see if you still have sound issues. If you are still having an issue, restore the sound to fix the issue.

- GO to your Start Menu. Search for the Device Manager.
- Expand out the Sound and Audio Devices.
- Right click on the sound driver, then you will choose uninstall.
- Click on the option Scan for Hardware Changes.
- Updated drivers will be automatically installed to your computer.

Fixing Your Display

Microsoft has designed and released the Microsoft Automated Troubleshooting Service, also known as ATS Fix It. It will allow you to detect and fix issues automatically that mess with your display quality and the text readability. Once you have downloaded the ATS Fix It and ran it, it will scan for the issues. You are able to choose to allow it to fix all the problems automatically or you can opt to select and then apply the fixes manually. Once the scan is complete, it will then present you will the report.

You will click on the option Next in order to fix all the issues. Once the issues are fixed, it will show a list down and inform you of the issues that has been fixes with your computer. Once the troubleshooting has been completed, and you have fixed the issues, you are able to restart your computer.

Chapter 4: How to Secure Windows 10 Systems

With every computer, there is an owner that would like to ensure that their computer is safe. Having a Windows 10 computer is no exception. In this chapter you are going to learn about the security features that this operating system has to offer. Biometric authentication and application vetting headline the security features of Windows 10.

Marc Maiffret, Windows security experts expressed that with Windows 10 security features with the combination of the Windows Store for authorized, as well as vetted application, Microsoft has made the desktop ecosystem looks more like a smartphone, which is great for security.

Device Guard

Microsoft's Device Guard is has aimed at blocking the zero day attacks by vetting the applications that will try to access the Windows 10 machine, as well as the network. It blocks any application that is not signed by certain software vendors, the enterprise itself, and the Windows app store.

Fujitsu, Acer, NCR, HP, Par, Lenovo, and Toshiba has teamed up with the company Microsoft to use the Device Guard on their devices that are Windows based.

It supports a point of sale system, ATM, and even other internet devices that run Windows.

In order to help protect the users from malware, once an app is executed, the program will make a determination on if the app is trustworthy, and it will notify the user if it is not. The Device Guard can use virtualization and hardware technology in order to isolate that decision making the function from the rest of the operating system, which will help provide addition protection from malware or attackers.

Privacy Settings

You are able to access the privacy settings using the Control Panel, which is titled Setting in this certain operating system. The fastest way that you can get there is by using the keyboard shortcut; Windows-I. Another method to get there is to tap your Windows key, which will open the Start menu, and then you will click the Settings button. You are also able to right click the button and then select Pin to Taskbar in order to create a shortcut for you to use later.

We will focus on the second to the last section in the Settings, which is labeled Privacy. Sine your Settings tool will bring you back to wherever you had left off, you may not see your Privacy button if you have been messing with the Settings. If that is the case, then you will click the back arrow in the left hand upper corner of your window to go to the home page.

Before you start messing with everything, here is a word of warning; although you have tempted to disable everything that will reduce the privacy, doing so may disable or impair some apps and the interactions between certain aps. If you find that this is an issue, you will have to come back and then re-enable things until the issue goes away. This can be a bit time consuming if you have made a lot of changes. Unfortunately, the Privacy section will not have a button to restore your default settings, so you will have to track the changes that you have made. It is recommended that you take screenshots of the sections before you make any changes.

General Pane

Clicking on your Privacy button will open a window that has two panes. On the left is your category list, and then on the right is the settings for the categories that you are looking at. In the General pane, there are settings listed. These are SmartScreen, advertising ID, and language.

Advertising ID identifies the Web behavior to deliver certain ads. If wikis in this manner: if you open your Windows 10 Travel app and also your Calendar app, Microsoft is able to use that information in order to show you certain ads. That is assuming that the app uses ads. You will not begin seeing banner ads when you open your calculator, but Microsoft Edge can run these certain ads once you go to Outlook.com or Bing.

However, it does not offer any personal information to the company about you. It is a bit like a beacon in order to deliver ads that are relevant to you so that you are more likely to click on them. It is to give you a better shopping experience.

The SmartScreen is a filter and is a layer that Internet Explorer and Microsoft Edge uses in order to help protect the computer from suspicious or dangerous websites. This filter does this in two different ways. One is that it analyzes the websites for any questionable behaviors like trying to open pop ups that are fake or redirecting you to another website. The second way is that it checks the address against a list that is maintained, which is a list of fraudulent sites. You will get a false positive once in awhile, but for the main part of surfing the net, you will be save and it is recommended that it is left on. The language setting will help websites detect what language that you are using so that they are able to deliver the language that you prefer.

Location Pane

If you are using the administrator account, then you will be able to see the option to disable the location information for all of the users on that specific device. Below that is the toggle that you can use for the specific account that is logged in, which will look grayed out if your location services are being disabled for everyone. Location can be used in order to let Windows 10 apps to display region specific information like sports scores and weather, or to show map locations and even shopping choices in your specific area. If you disable the setting, you are still able to enter the location information in manually, id just will not be sent to you automatically.

There are some apps that will use the device's Bluetooth or the Wi-Fi functions in order to determine the location even when the location setting is not being used. You are able to toggle that feature on and off in your Radios pane. Bluetooth and Wi-Fi will still be able to function, just without the location information.

Camera and Microphone

As you have probably guessed, these sections include a toggle that will disable the webcam and your mic. You are also able to toggle certain apps, including the apps that are pre-installed and designed by Microsoft and the apps that you have also installed to replace these. If you have purchased the device from a builder like Acer, Dell, Lenovo, or Toshiba, they may even have some pre-installed apps too.

By default, Windows 10 apps get permissions for the camera and the mic regardless if you are going to use it, so it is recommended that you check the settings here and there if you are leaving the camera enabled. Typically, you should only give the camera and the mic access when you know that you will be using the app, like HipChat or Skype. Note that disabling the camera and the mic in your Settings may not prevent the malware from secretly enabling it again, and it will not have any effect on the operating system that you may be using to dual boot. You may want to put a piece of tape or something to that effect over your camera when you are not using it.

Inking, Speech, and Typing

The speech section is where you are able to toggle Cortana's speech recognition, among some other things. Cortana is like the loved Apple's Siri. However, it works on your desktop, as well as on the mobile devices. You are able to use the speech recognition in order to dictate your emails and more. Enabling this setting also improves other settings.

http://www.darkreading.com/cloud/microsoft-windows-10-three-security-features-to-know-about/d/d-id/1320650
http://download.cnet.com/blog/download-blog/a-guide-to-windows-10-security-settings/
http://download.cnet.com/blog/download-blog/windows-10-privacy-settings/

Chapter 5: How to Use the Registry Editor to Manage Hardware and Software Issues in Windows 10

Windows Registry is deemed a hierarchical database that offers the entire configuration and the settings that is used by series, components, applications, and most of everything on the system. The registry has two main concepts that you should know. They are Values and Keys. The Values are somewhat like files inside of a folder, and they offer actual settings. Registry Keys are the objects that are folder, and in your interface it looks like actual folders.

When you open up your Registry Editor, you will see a tree type view on the left side of the pane and it will contain all of your keys, with values on your right side. It is about as simple as it can get.

The root level keys that you are seeing on the left side are very important. Each one will house different sets of information, so you will need to know which of the sections that you need to go into. The interesting thing that people do not know about is that there are three of the five items on this root level are not actually there, they are linked to the items further down in one of the keys.

HKEY_CLASSES_ROOT

Windows uses this specific section in order to manage file type association, and it typically abbreviated HKCR when being references in a document. This key is actually a link that is to HKLM\Software\Classes.

HKEY_CURRENT_USER

This holds the user settings for certain logged in users, and it is normally abbreviated HKCU. This is really linked to HKEY_USERS\<SID-FOR-CURRENT-USER>. The crucial sub key in this section is HKCU\Software, which has the user level settings for most of the software.

HKEY_LOCAL_MACHINE

All of your system wide settings are here, and it is normally abbreviated as HKLM. You will use the HKLM\Software key mostly in order to check the machine wide settings.

HKEY_USERS

Stores all of your settings for the users on the system. You will normally use HKCU instead; however, if you want to check the settings for another user on the computer, you are able to use this one.

HKEY_CURRENT_CONFIG

This stores all of your information about the current configuration of the hardware. This one is not used often, and it is a link to

HKLM\SYSTEM\CurrentControlSet\Hardware Profiles\Current.

Creating New Values and Keys

If you right click on any of the keys in the left side of your window and will give you options, most of them are pretty straightforward and very easy to understand. You are able to create a new Key, which will then show up as a folder on the left side, or a new value, which will be on the right side. Those values are a bit confusing. However, there are only a couple of the values that you will use regularly.

- String value - REG_SZ: This has anything that will fit into a string. Much of the time, you are able to edit the human readable strings without breaking something.
- Binary Value - REG_BINARY: This value has arbitrary binary data, and you will probably never edit this one.
- DWORD - 32 bit, Value - REG_DWORD: These are always used for the regular integer value, no matter if it is a 0 or 1, or even a number from 0 all the way up to 4, 294, 967, 295.
- QWORD 64 bit, Value - REG_QWORD: These are not used most of the time for any registry hacking, but it is basically a 64 bit integer value.
- Multi-String Value - REG_MULTI_SZ: These are the values that are fairly uncommon however, it works like a notepad in a window. You are able to type multi-line textual information into a field.

- Expandable String Value - REG_EXPAND_SZ: These are the variables that have a string that is able to contain environment variables and often times is used for the system paths. A string may be %SystemDrive%\Windows and will expand to C:\Windows. This will mean that once you find a value in the Registry that is this type, you are able to insert or change the environment variable and they will then expand before the string is used.

Favorites Menu

One of the most useful features that no one seems to even notice is the Favorites menu, which is wonderful when you want to check a location of a registry regularly. What is even more great than that is that you are able to export the list of the favorites and then use it again on a different computer without having to browse the keys and then add them to the menu. It is also a nice way to bookmark something that is in the registry if you want to look around in many different location, so you are able to easily flip back to the last one your were at.

Exporting Registry Files

You are able to export registry keys and all of your values contained under them by right clicking on the key and then choosing Export. This is important if you are getting ready to making any changes to the system. Once you have gotten the exported registry file, you are able to double click on it in order to enter the information back into your registry, or you are able to choose Edit to use Notepad to look at the contents.

Setting Permissions

Some of your registry keys will not allow you to make any changes by default. This is typically because you do not have any permissions to those keys; however, you are able to tweak the permission if you want just by right clicking on the key and then choosing Permissions, and then you need to adjust them from there.

Loading Registry Hives

You are able to use the path File, then Load Hive feature to load up a specific registry from another system. Perhaps you need to troubleshoot another system, and you would like to see what is going on in your registry for the system that is not booting. So you will boot the system from your rescue dick, or maybe using a Linux live CD, and then you will copy your registry files onto the thumb drive. Now you are able to open up a computer in order to look around by using the Load Hive feature.

Chapter 6: Installation Options for Windows 10

In this chapter you are going to learn how to install Windows 10 and the options that you will have. Before you do something to your computer, the rule of thumb is to back it up. Ensure that all of your data is backed up. There are three different ways that you can get Windows 10. You can purchase a newer PC with it preloaded, purchase a licensed copy online, or by upgrading your existing computer.

When you go to install this operating system, you will see a greeting that says, "Get going fast... change these at any time". However, it is highly suggested that if you care about your privacy, you will need to customize it, and choose not to go fast.

- **Personalization**: This will personalize your typing, speech, and inking input by sending the contacts and the calendar details along with other input data to the company Microsoft. Sent inking and typing data to Microsoft to improve upon the recognition and the suggestion platform It will let apps use the advertising ID for across apps. Location is on due to default unless you manually change it.
- **Browser and Protection**: SmartScreen online will help protect you against the malicious

content and any download in the websites that are loaded by Windows Store apps and browsers. Use the page prediction in order to improve the reading, speed up your browser, and make the overall experience better in the browser. The browsing data will be sent to the company.

- **Connectivity and Error Reporting**: The computer will automatically connect to the suggested hotspots, even though all of the networks are not secure. It will also automatically connect to any shared networks that are on your contacts. It will send errors and diagnostic information to the company.
- **Applications**: On this screen you will choose the default apps that you would have to accept if you did the fast install. Here you are able to choose the applications that you actually want.

Chapter 7: How to Upgrade to Windows 10

In this chapter you will learn how to upgrade your computer to Windows 10. Just because it is an easy process, it does not meant that there are not things that you need to do before you go upgrading and the important choices to make while you upgrading. While there are many websites that point a person to the installer and telling them that they just need to download it and run it, you should take the time in order to give you a chance to use these tips.

What You Need

In order to upgrade your computer from Windows 7 or Windows 8 up to Windows 10, there is a very small list of things that you must have and a few that are recommended. Here is what you are going to need before moving ahead and then some of the best practices highlighted.

- **Activated Copy of Windows 10**: The most important aspect of this is the current version of Windows is activated properly. Although Microsoft has alluded to the idea that this operating system would be a large sweeping upgrade that would install on even a pirated copy of Windows that plan never really came to pass and you need to have an activated copy. In order to check if the copy is activated, press the

Windows Key + W in order to pull up your Setting search and then type in Activated in order to access the "See if Windows is Activated" menu. You can also look under the Control Panel, System in order to see your status.

- **Appropriate Windows 10 Update Tool**: ALthough the update tool is straight forward, you will need to right version for the hardware. The first step is to determine if you are running a 32 bit or 64 bit machine. You are able to check what version you are running by looking in the same panel as the activated panel above.
- **Running Upgrade Installer**: You will first be prompted to upgrade your computer or create an installation media for another computer. Select the option 'Upgrade this PC now' in order to begin your upgrading process. Click the Next button. This will begin the download process, which is short or long depending on your connection to the internet. When it is finished download and also unpacking the installation media you will be prompted to accept the terms of your new license agreement. You will need to click 'Accept' and then the installer will do an update check before moving over to a confirmation page.

By default, the installer selects the largest selection of 'what to keep'. If you would like to make changes to what you are keeping, click the small button 'change what to keep'. You will be prompted to select what type of installation you would like.

When you are ready, click on the Next button in order to proceed and then it will return you to final screen. Confirm that you are ready to go and it will show what you would like. After confirming your installation, click the Install page. The PC will then reboot a few times as your installer works and when it is done you will be returned to the login screen.

Configure Windows After Upgrade

When you get to the login screen for the first time, you are not done yet. There are some little tweaks that you can do before you boot into Windows. You should take advantage of them. As soon as you have logged in for the very first time you will be prompted to choose between Customize settings or Express Settings. You need to click on ' Customize Settings in order to see what has been set to default and confirm if you want them or not.

Chapter 8: Windows 10 Configuration to Protect Privacy

Everyone needs to protect private data. Whether you are carrying sensitive files for work, passwords, or sensitive pictures, there is specific information that you do not want anyone else to have. When you are setting up the computer, you are establishing habits that you are going to use through the time of the computer. Rather than waiting to care about the privacy settings later, it is better to do it now.

Before doing anything to your computer, you need to make sure that you are starting from a clean slate. If you have purchased your computer from the store, it probably came with a lot of software that is junk. Get rid of the junk in order to keep your computer running smooth. There is also software that can be intrusive.

- Wipe the computer and reinstall your operating system from scratch. This is one way to ensure that there is no extra junk on your system. If you have built your own computer, you are probably okay with this. If you are running a bought system, be sure to keep track of your license key before you do this.
- Remove any bloatware manually. It is a bit more of a process that is tedious, and it is possible to accidentally leave items behind, but it will allow

you to clean your system without wiping it out completely.

A clean install is a great step in order to take regardless of if you are concerned about privacy or not. However, to make sure that there is nothing on the system that makes your data vulbernalbe, it is even more crucial. The only way to do this and be sure is to clear out everything when you first set up the computer.

Audit Your Privacy Section of Settings App

With the operating system Windows 8, Microsoft introduced the new style of apps. To go with this, Microsoft has also added a new system for permissions. This is geared towards tablets and phones, but as this company steers developers towards their store, there are more apps that are more likely to use the permissions in order to access things like the microphone, camera, or your location. In order to manage this permission, you will need to open the Start menus and type in 'privacy', and then choose the Privacy Settings. Here are the settings that you should tweak:

- **Location**: You are able to set your location that all of the apps will use, or you can disable the location tracking completely. You are also able to see a list of the apps that have the ability to use the location and disable or enable them per app.

- **Camera and Microphone**: You are able to block any access to the camera or your microphone per app, or you can disable the access completely. Just like the location settings, this section only will apply in the modern app style. It also will not disable any devices on the system level.
- **Calendar, Contacts, and Messages**: If you are using any services from Microsoft that manages your events, contacts, or your messages, you are able to control which of the apps has access to the data.
- **Typing and Speech**: Under this you are able to disable the "get to know me" feature. This setting is placed a bit weird and it is unclear how much data is tracked with this one, but it does say that it is used to offer better suggestions, improve your dictation, and will help Cortana to get to know you. So, if you are not comfortable with this digital assistant learning your specific habits, it might be best to just turn it off.

Depending on how much you want the operating system to know about you specifically, it will be worth going through the Privacy section. Also, you need to keep in mind that any of the permission you will disable here only apply to your apps that are displayed. Microsoft's permission system is a bit new, so unless you have downloaded an app from the store, this probably will not prevent them from actually using your hardware.

Chapter 9: Guide to Windows 10 Backup

Once you have installed Windows 10 onto your computer, and you have installed all of the drivers that you need, as well as configuring your settings; the next step is to back up your computer and all of the settings. You are able to do this by creating an image backup of the system drive and storing it on a different partition on your local hard drive, a network location, or even a DVD. If anything ever goes wrong with your computer while you are working with it, you are able to revert right back to the previous state in just minutes. Here is how you will back up your computer:

- Log onto your computer through the administrator account.
- Once you have arrived to the desktop, right click on your Start button.
- From this menu, click on the Control Panel.
- In the Control Panel window, you will need to ensure you click 'View by' type is set on Category.
- Click on the 'System and Security' category, and then from this window, click on Security and Maintenance.
- From the bottom of the pane on the left, click on the File History link.
- Again, from the bottom of the pane to the left, click on System Image Backup.

- On this opened Create a System Image window, from the available buttons representing the corresponding options.
- Select the way you would like to save the backup file.
- Once you have selected the location, follow your on screen instruction in order to create the image backup.

Chapter 10: Restore and Recovery

You have upgraded to the Windows 10 operating system. But once you have made your change, you will want to ensure that you are able to backup and restore the data fast and conveniently. The Factory Reset and System Restore has been included into Windows 10, and are much better than they were with the operating system Windows 8.

No Recovery Partition

Microsoft is extremely confident in the refresh, restore, and reset tools that they have packaged into this version of Windows that there isn't a recovery partition. Whereas in the operating system Windows 8 you were able to use the recovery image on a hidden partition in order to restore the system, this is no longer an option. The reason behind this is to allow the user to maximize on the available disk space, which in conjunction with this file compression will save more than 6 GB on a 64 bit system that is running Windows 10. This will offer a large advantage to those will a small capacity of system.

As the partition was the nearest to having the installation media, this is not ideal. However, the refresh and the reset tools should be good enough to deal with any major issues, as long as you are making the right decisions between refreshing and restoring Windows.

Using the System Restore

If you are having problems with Windows 10's performance, the very first thing that you should look at is the list of the restore points. If one of these points coincides with the point in which the system began to misbehave, then you are able to use the System Restore tool in order to reinstate the setting and the software that were in place during this time.

You will need to open Start, then settings. You will then search the box type with create a restore point. Click on the matching result, select your drive that you would like to use in order to use for your restore point. Click on Configure, then Turn on System Protection. This action will activate the system restore functionality. Click on the OK button to confirm your choice, and then in the main window you will click on Create. This will create a restore point and you will then give it a name.

The system protection software will then create a restore point, which you are able to revert to later should you need to. You might need to spend just a few moments checking through the items that will be affected so that you are able to reinstall any software and avoid any apps that may have caused the issues.

Refresh a Windows 10 Computer

If reverting to a restore point did not resolve the issues with the computer, then you will need to refresh the setting. This will revert the system to a similar state to what it was when you had bought the computer. The only difference is that you be able to keep your data and your settings.

Open up Start, then Settings; once there you will click on Update & Security in order to begin. Select Recovery in the left menu. Under the 'Reset this PC', you will click or tap 'Get Started. You will then use the Keep my Files option. A warning will be shown, and a second might appear if you have upgraded to this operating system.

Reset Windows 10

There may come a time when you have to completely set your computer back to all of its original settings. This is much like a tablet or a smartphone. This action will restore the system to factory settings and it will leave it like new. You will need to backup any data that you need to keep.

You will need to go back to the Reset this PC option, and then click on Get Started. This time, you will not keep your files, you will select the option Remove Everything. Here you will have two different options; Just Remove My Files for quick reset and Remove Files and Clean Drive. The last option will take much longer, but it is the most secure; therefore, making it more useful for wiping your system clean before you sell it or give it away.

Chapter 11: Security of the New Windows 10

With good protection at the core, Windows 10 is by far the most secure of Windows ever. From the virtualization based security all the way to Windows Hello and Enterprise Data Protection, this operating system has concentrated on security, along with other modern features. Most of the issues that you hear other computer owners expressing concern for is covered by Windows 10 automatically by default. This operating system has many new features that have your security in mind.

Virtualization Based Security

You cannot talk about the security of this operating system without discussing the large, underlying security architecture that has been added known as the virtualization based security, also known as VBS. VBS uses certain software and hardware enforced mechanisms in order to create an isolated, hypervisor restricted, securing, specialized subsystem for storing, transferring, and operating other very sensitive subsystems and data.

VBS makes it extremely hard for any attacker to mess with the core components of your operating system. VBS is not just an improved defense, it represents the entire architectural change that largely reduces the surface area of attack and attempt to eliminate any attack vector. All malware and hacking will not just magically go away, but the VBS will create a secure environment where the parts of the operating system is far less likely to be tampered with, and the critical data is much less likely to be reused or stolen.

Secure Booting

If you are worried about rootkits and any other low level malware; don't. In this operating system, Windows 10 offers an impossible machine for hackers to break into thanks to the secure booting.

Windows Vista had inaugurated the secure booting. It had used BitLocker and TPM chip in order to protect the booting process. Windows 7 then debuted Unified Extensible Firmware Interface, which had replaced the highly vulnerable traditional BIOS, and then Windows 8 had incorporated the secure boot protections by adding in the newer UEFI version. Windows and UEFI work together in order to make sure that the hardware and the lowest levels of the operating system are not tampered with. If there should be any tampering, you will get a warning or an unauthorized modification is prevented.

Debuting in the Windows 8, a feature that is called Windows Trusted Boot offers code integrity validation that offered protections for all of the Windows boot function from any tampering and automatically remediates if the tampering is found. In addition, it also included an early launch anti malware capability, which had ensured the antimalware software began before the malware could launch. In the previous versions of Microsoft's Windows, malware could begin before the AV and was able to tamper with the functions. However, you still needed to ensure that the preferred anti malware software had supported ELAM.

Windows Hello

Windows Hello is an attempt to get rid of the passwords, which is often wimes stolen and also reused. Hello supports three different methods of biometric authentication, which is the fingerprint, face, and iris; in concert with a PIN.

Many devices and computers that are purchased today support Windows Hello, and the devices that detect the biometric identifiers has been tested to make sure that they cannot easily be hacked. Microsoft worked hard with the members of the Chaos Computing Club, which had experienced hacking biometric devices.

Hello is only for logons. The stored information will never leave the device, and even is an attacker takes it, it would just be useless on any other device. Once you are successfully authenticated using this software, the newer Passport authentication mechanism can be used.

Passport

Microsoft Passport is a single sign on solution that is advanced and has little to do with the option from a year ago. Behind the scenes, this software supports the open FIDO Alliance and it works with a public key cryptography, although you do not need PKI in order to use it. From the behind the scenes technical perspective, it actually works like a smart card, but it does not need a separate card or a card reader.

If the computer has a TPM chip, the private key of your asymmetric key pair is also securely stored there instead of being inside the software. You use the PIN or Hello in order to authenticate locally, then you will use Passport in order to securely authenticate to a different network location. Passport also works with the enterprise Active Directory, Microsoft account, Azure Active Directory, or any other FIDO identity provider.

Credential Guard

If you are worried about the pass the hash attacks, then you will need to implement the Credential Guard. It will protect the authentication broker and the user's derived credentials in the VBS. This is done by isolating the authentication service, as well as protecting the NTLM credential data.

On the downside, this does not protect the local credentials, which are located in the registry or on the local disk. It does not currently work with the Remote

Desktop Protocol logons. However, if you ensure that the local administrative passwords are unique between the computers, then the typical password attacker will be slowed or stopped.

Device Guard

Device Guard is a highly secure tool that will determine which of the applications and scripts should be able to run on a certain computer. Windows had had a close feature since the Windows XP operating system, which has since improved with AppLocker. However, Device Guard uses hardware power in order to protect the integrity of what is and is not allowed to run on the computer. Companies and even vendors are able to add the approved software to the list of the applications that are allowed to run. If used properly, it can even prevent most of the maliciousness from happening. Microsoft also recommends that you use Device Guard, as well as AppLocker.

Enterprise Data Protection

BitLocker protects the data when the device is stolen or lost, however, how do you protect it from those users who may accidentally leak the data? This is where a feature of Windows 10 comes in. It is called Enterprise Data Protection. It provides persistent file level encryption and the basic rights management to corporate the files.

Enterprise Data Protection does not get in any way of the experience using the computer. You are able to continue to use the apps that you like or even choose access protected content. Those users that are not required to work with the special folders, move into secure partitions or zones, or change modes. Windows acts like a broker that gates the user and the app access to a protected data based policy that you have defined.

Enterprise Data Protection is an amazing program that identifies, protects, and separates data. In many cases it is able to do so without any need for app wrapping or reengineering. EDP can be used in combination with the Rights Management and Azure Active Directory services to offer secure B to B sharing.

Miscellaneous Features

There are so many tiny changes that actually make a Windows 10 computer more or easier to secure. For example, DMA Attack Mitigation, the EMET enabled protections, and the ability to prevent local accounts from logging on over a network. Also, do not forget that the security options that are available in other versions of Windows include Account Control, Kerberos Armoring, TPM Key Attestation, SmartScreen, Advance Auditing, and so much more.

Chapter 12: Choosing the Best Anti-Virus

Consumer antivirus programs or software is much like purchasing an insurance policy. It is arguably the most crucial program that you will install on your computer, yet it is often the very last program a user ever wants to purchase or use. Another similar feature between the insurance and the antivirus software is what is also called a risk.

Nowadays, no matter if it is free, expensive, built in, or compare, the best antivirus program will depend on the level of risk that the user will undergo. Those that are really at risk might feel a bit more comfortable with a top shelf, higher priced program, whereas the person who has less concern may just want to download a free program.

Although Windows 10 offers an antivirus, which is called Windows Defender, the fact of the matter is there are many people who want another anti-virus.
- If you absolutely want the best protection: You are going to have to pay more. Kaspersky is a highly ranked program that has passed various different antivirus tests, and the interface is very user friendly.
- If you need the best free protection: You are able to examine the ranking on your own in order to see the best of the free options; however, Avira Free Antivirus offers the best balance between

the non instructions and the protection. It normally scores pretty high for protection.

- If you would like the least intrusive of the free protection options: Windows Defender will not trick you into installing something that you do not want. It will never nag with any ads. If you care about intrusiveness more than you do about the protection, Windows Defender is a good option. Windows Defender automatically disables itself when you install another third party antivirus. It will re-enable again if you uninstall that antivirus. It is designed to get out of your way, yet not leave you vulnerable.

Having an antivirus is pretty important; however, these days it is more important that you use a good program to protect the web browser and the plug ins, which are the biggest targets for attackers now. MalwareBytes Anti-Exploit is a free program that is highly recommended. It functions very similar to the EMET security tool, but it is more friendly to the user and it offers more security features. This will help block common exploit techniques.

While you are getting and installing protective software, it is recommended to download MalwareBytes Anti-Malware. It is a good and solid anti-malware program that functions great with an antivirus and an anti-exploit program. It will find a lot the junkware that is typically forgotten by the anti-virus.

Those who would like a specific Antivirus for Windows and need a free option, you need to download Avira. It is free and is specifically created for Window operating machines. Here is a list of the features that you get with this free program:

- Scanning detects the threats in real time from the files as you are using them.
- Starts a full system scan on your demand.
- Schedules updates and scans when you would like.
- You can manage the firewall setting right in Avira.
- You are able to view event logs in order to help analyze any threats.
- It has won awards for the real world protection, overall performance, file detection, as well as malware removal.

This program is tested rigorously every year. It has stood out in many key areas. I has received awards in different areas, overall, it has been set forward and the number one free app for security. Avira had also taken home awards from the AV Test in the year 2015. It received the top ranking spot for usability for two years in a row, and now has also won for the best repair tool, even over Malwarebytes.

Avira earns the usability awards as well. While it is not quite set and forget it programs, it is very close. After you have installed it, Avira will set to run a system scan every seven days. The real time feature will be active too. If you would like to perform or even schedule a full scan you will need to do it manually. It is a great idea to run at least one deep scan as soon as you open the program for the first time.

Chapter 13: Windows 10 and Your Printer

In this chapter you are going to learn how to get your printer to work with your computer that is now running Windows 10. Most printers that are connected to computers are using a USB port and they often work just by plugging them in. A new printer can also come with specific driver that is located on a disc. Here is how you will add your printer to your computer:

- You will sign in on your computer through the administrator account.
- Connect the printing device to your computer.
- Click on the Start button on the desktop screen.
- From there you will click on Settings.
- In the Settings window, you will click on Devices.
- Once this window is open, on the left pane, ensure that the select the category Printers & Scanners.
- From the right, under the Add Printers and Scanners section, you will click on Add a Printer or Scanner.
- You will wait while the computer searched for the printer that is connected. If the computer finds your printer, you are able to click on the name and then follow the instructions on the screen in order to finish the installation process. If the computer fails to detect your printer, then you will continue with the steps.

- If the computer can't detect the printer, click on the printer that I want is not listed.
- On the option Find a printer with other options, click on the Add a local printer or network printer with manual settings button.
- Click on the Next button.
- On the window Choose a printer port, leave the default options chosen, and then click on the Next button. If you are advanced, you can also just choose a different option from the drop down list; Use an existing port.
- On the window Install the Printer Driver, from your displayed list of manufacturers of printers, click in order to select the one that you have connected to your computer.
- From the right side, locate your model and click it.
- Click on the next button.
- Continue through selecting your correct options.
- Type in the name of the printer and then click on the next button.
- On the window Printer Sharing, ensure that the Share This Printer so that other... button is selected. Continue on until you get to finish.

Conclusion:

Windows 10 is a modern style of a classic operating system that has made its home inside of yours. It is a household name, brand, and system. From the beginning all the way to this upgraded "Perfect 10", this system has a lot to offer from features to style. Learn what this system has to offer and you will be able to keep sensitive information safe and add functionality, along with organization into your life. From the special security features all the way to the ease of use, you will surely fall in love with Windows Thank you again for downloading this book!

I hope this book was able to help you find better sense of windows 10

Finally, if you enjoyed this book, then I'd like to ask you for a favor, would you be kind enough to leave a review for this book on Amazon? It'd be greatly appreciated!

Thank you and good luck!

HACKING:

The Ultimate Beginners Guide to the World of HACKING

circumstances will any legal responsibility or blame be held against the publisher for any reparation, damages, or monetary loss due to the information herein, either directly or indirectly.

Respective authors own all copyrights not held by the publisher.

The information herein is offered for informational purposes solely, and is universal as so. The presentation of the information is without contract or any type of guarantee assurance.

The trademarks that are used are without any consent, and the publication of the trademark is without permission or backing by the trademark owner. All trademarks and brands within this book are for clarifying purposes only and are the owned by the owners themselves, not affiliated with this document.

Table of Contents:

Introduction

Congratulations for downloading the book, "The Ultimate Beginners Guide to the World of HACKING

Always wondered what Black Hat means when it comes up over and over again on the telly maybe as you were watching or maybe you've heard the term malware or actually experience the frustration of your browser opening without reason. Well this is the book for you .This book contain the basic concepts utilized in the hacking world. In this book you will undergo 14 chapters that will lead you behind the scenes of the different software used, equipment and tools used to perform ethical hacks and prevent cyber-attacks.

Thank you for downloading this book and I

hope you find the content most useful

Chapter 1

What is Hacking?

In the world of information technology (IT), hacking is the manipulation of the normal behavior of network connections, systems and computer software. A hacker is one who breaks passwords and codes to gain unauthorized entry into computer systems. Hacking is typically associated with malicious attacks on the Internet and private networks. This is largely due to well-publicized hacks that have caused huge amounts of damage to government, corporate, and personal computing systems. Many hackers often do not aim to cause damage or steal information, they simply enjoy the challenge of breaking into systems. In some cases, however, a hacker's intention could be to deceive, steal valuable information, or to damage a network. The majority of hacking attacks are launched by disgruntled employees. They tend to have access to passwords and User IDs which makes their hacking significantly easier.

Malicious hackers are referred to as "Black Hat" or criminal hackers. This describes individuals who illegally break into computer systems to harm or capture information. Despite the general public perceiving that all hackers are malicious, most hackers are actually people who are interested in how computers, networks, and programs function and are often simply learning and exploring.

Common Network Hacking Techniques

Hacking networks is often achieve through scripts or other programs. These programs are able to access and control data traveling throughout the network. A variety of pre-packaged scripts are available on the Internet for everyone, usually "Noobs" (entry-level hackers), to use. More experienced hackers may enhance these scripts to develop new capabilities. A select few expert hackers get employed by commercial firms and governments to protect the organization's software and secure information from outside hackers.

Networks are usually penetrated through a 'backdoor' program installed on infected computers. You can defend yourself from attacks by using a firewall and an updated anti-virus program. Backdoor programs often arrive through opened email attachments containing the backdoor malware. It is common for such a programs to send copies of itself to everyone on your email contact list. It is therefore possible for a friend to send you a malicious program unknowingly.

Good hacking requires a combination of personality traits and technical skills. Hackers should be able to work well with math. They should have the ability to assemble facts and details that may come from a variety of disparate sources. They should also have the organizational skills to strategically plan out an attack. If this sounds like you, then you have come to the right place! This eBook provides an informative introduction to the world of ethical hacking.

Chapter 2

Classifications of Hackers

Hackers is an umbrella term that has come to define individuals or groups who use nonstandard methods to gain access to information stored in technology or to control the technology itself. What distinguishes on hacker from another is not the methodology, but the intent of the hacker. Here we categorize hackers based on the intent of their actions.

Script Kiddie

Script Kiddies are a hacking amateurs who have neither formal training in computer science nor particularly-good amateur skills. These hackers are characterized by lack of interest in becoming advanced hackers. Equipped with minimal technology skills, these hackers typically download user-friendly hacking tools (such as vulnerability scanners) with graphic user interfaces (GUIs) that guide them through the process. Attacks launched by script kiddies are usually minor and, due to careless work, rife with incriminating digital fingerprints. Script Kiddies are known to launch attacks for personal amusement.

Green Hats

Green Hat hackers (also referred to as a "Noobs") are inexperienced hackers working toward hacking proficiency. These hackers launch attacks for the purpose of learning. Green Hats tend to use the same tools as the Script Kiddies, and engage in similarly low-level attacks. What most distinguishes this group from the Script Kiddies is the motivation behind their attacks.

Blue Hats

Blue Hat hackers are independent computer security specialists that are hired by software companies to bug test a systems before they go to market. These hackers search for vulnerabilities in a system so that they can be patched.

Red Hats

Red Hat hackers are considered the vigilantes of the hacker community. Similar to White Hats, these hackers work to protect a system. When they encounter someone attempting to breach their system, however, they launch malicious counterattacks, sending back viruses to the intruder. Red Hats are typically advanced hackers who may use sophisticated techniques to accomplish their attacks.

White Hats

White Hat hackers (also known as an Ethical Hackers) are computer network security specialists who break into private, secured networks with non-malicious intent. A White Hat hacker has expert understanding of computer network architecture, network protocols, and structured network management. White Hats employ a continually-evolving arsenal of technology tools to protect private networks from outside malicious attacks. This includes a variety of open-source hacking tools and custom tools they program themselves. These hackers have the ability to break into networks, but use their skills to help identify and patch security holes. White Hats are usually hired by businesses and governments to conduct penetration tests for network vulnerabilities in order to formulate network defense assessments test and patch holes that could be exploited by intruders. White Hat hackers are considered the "good guys" of the hacking community. The majority of White Hats have formal training in computer science and obtain specialized certifications to qualify them for the mainstream job market.

Gray Hats

Gray (sometimes spelled "Grey") Hats are the largest group in the hacking world. These hackers occasionally conduct both white and black hacking activities, depending on what they're trying to accomplish or who's paying them. For the most part, Gray Hat attacks are limited to nuisances that do not result in loss of money or significant violations damage to the target.

Black Hats

Black Hat hackers (also known as "Crackers") launch clandestine attacks, lacking permission to be on a network or authorization to conduct certain activities. The goal of most Black Hats is to access sensitive financial data for the purpose of stealing money. Advanced Black Hats are able to breach systems and cover their tracks. They sometimes stage attacks to make it appear as though someone else is responsible. Black Hats are often form secretive collectives through which they share information and cooperate on attacks.

State Sponsored Hackers

National governments recruit and employ hackers to help find and patch vulnerabilities in official and classified networks. The skills involved with penetration testing one nation's government network, however, naturally extend to penetration testing opposing governments' network systems. Virtually all governments have incorporated state-sponsored hacking into their overall military strategies. China, for example, has an entire cyber hacking division in their military. The U.S. has also been accused of sponsoring cyber-attacks on other nations. Such attacks include threats to government infrastructures and cyber spying. In the 21st century, "cyber security" has become synonymous with "national security."

Spy Hackers

Spy Hackers are hired by governments and private businesses to help acquire access to various forms of confidential information from their competitors. These hackers are commissioned to penetrate government network security systems to access secret files and access classified materials about, for example, weapons development and names of international secret agents. Corporate Spy hackers may hack in from the outside or gain employment in order to act as a mole.

Hacktivists

Hacktivism is a concept that brings together hacking and social or political activism. Hacktivists exist at all skill levels and have historically deployed attacks that deface websites, temporarily shut down networks, or effect significant inconveniences, all without causing destruction or substantially harming the target. Hacktivists on more extreme ends of the spectrum have been known to release secret and officially classified information to the public. Extreme hacktivists are sometimes considered to be cyber terrorists by those receiving the attacks.

Cyber Terrorists
     Hacking for the purpose of causing fear, bodily harm, or destruction of property is considered cyber terrorism. Although hacking takes place in the virtual world, it can result in physical consequences. Shutting down a hospital system or disrupting critical medical records in its database could result in the death of patients. Hacking attacks that disable power grids or traffic control systems could cause a great deal of physical destruction. Exposing personal information, such as lists of names and addresses could be place individuals in danger. Cyber terrorism is an extreme form of Black Hat activity.

     This categorization of hackers is not exhaustive. There are many ways in which hackers are categorized, and many more ways in which hackers categorize themselves. This list, however, is comprehensive in its description of hacker activity in general and a useful means for conceptualizing the mysterious world of hacking.

Chapter 3

Types of Attacks

It is common practice for groups of experienced crackers and even amateur hackers to successfully steal secure data from millions of computers every day. The strategies today are essentially the same as they have always been: to trick targets into revealing sensitive information, to steal passwords, and to install malicious software on target computers. Here I discuss the most common types of attacks.

<u>Malware</u>

Malware is an inclusive term for an assortment of dangerous software programs, including: sneak-ware, adware, key-loggers, browser hijackers, porn servers, Trojans, and worms. Essentially, malware is code with harmful intent designed to steal data or disable parts of a device. Once installed, malware can create countless problems for the computer. This type of program can record keystrokes, capture passwords, monitor browser activity, force windows to open, flood email with spam, redirect web browsers, and many other operations that may not only be frustrating, but costly. These programs will function without the user's knowledge. Malvertising is a virus-infected display advertisement that downloads malware when a user clicks on it. These programs are usually difficult to without the use of special tools or a clean wipe of the hard drive. Rogue security software impersonates authentic security software for protecting your computer. Programmers design alerts and pop-up windows that recommend the user to download infected software.

Phishing

Like Spam, phishing attacks are introduced through email. The target is prompted to click on a link, and the link directs the user to a counterfeit website. The user is then prompted to enter log-in credentials, therefore compromising the user's identification and password. In some cases, all a user has to do is click on the link. Phishing (so named for its use of lures to hook a target into revealing confidential information) describes efforts to deceptively attain private information, such as login credentials and bank information, details, by impersonating legitimate individuals, businesses, or government entities. The purpose of phishing is to gain access to enough information to impersonate the victim for a variety of nefarious purposes. Victims can be selected arbitrarily or specifically targeted.

Password Attacks

Unlike malware, the tools used to hack passwords do not need to be installed on the target computer. Methods that hackers widely employ include: Brute Force, Password Resetting, and Cracking.

Password Guessing

Hackers can use automated programs to assist them with guessing passwords. Such programs can rapidly enter logical sequences of passwords until the eventually stumble upon the correct one. Dictionary hacks submit complete words, dates, and numbers. These tools utilize dictionary databases. Hybrid password guessing software combines uppercase and lowercase characters, spells words in unconventional ways, and includes non-alphanumeric special characters.

Password Resetting

Hackers can physically booting the computer from an external drive, which allows them to bypass the operating system's security settings, and reset the computer.

Password Cracking

Password cracking involves taking a captured password hash and converting it to its plain text original. This is accomplished with the help of tools designed for sniffing and extracting authentication information. Specially-designed hacking tools can "sniff" authentication transmissions and retrieve useful password information.

Password Capturing

Complete passwords can be extracted through a keyboard-logging virus installed on the target machine or by connecting a small physical device designed to record keyboard strokes.

Distributed Denial-of-Service (DDoS) Attacks

A DDoS attack is designed to disrupt or completely shut down a network. The hacker does employs any number of techniques to cause the network to fail. The type attack involves coordination of many computers within the network simultaneously cooperating in a way that overloads or disrupts network, causing the system to malfunction.

"Man in the Middle" (MITM)

The MITM attack involve the hacker breaking into a connection, usually through an unencrypted wireless access point (WAP) and impersonates each person to the other. In this way, the attacker may gain access to sensitive data from both participants.

Drive-By Downloads

Drive-by downloads occur when a user visits a typical website and unwittingly downloads a snippet of code, which is a small part of a larger program. This partial program then communicates with other computers online and installs the rest of its script, making it a complete program. This creates problems by finding weaknesses in the target computer or in vulnerable programs installed on the machine.

Today's hackers continuously develop innovative ways lure clients into a false sense of security. Using fake public wireless access points, running banner ad infected with malware, offering free software downloads containing harmful scripts, and creating counterfeit websites from which to capture login credentials are simply new ways to accomplish the familiar goals of stealing information and taking control of target machines.

Chapter 4
Hacking Tools

Included in this chapter is a variety of commonly-used hacking tools. To keep this simple for the beginning hacker, this chapter focuses on a popular free, open-source complete hacking bundle. Kali Linux is a Linux distribution designed for security scanning and penetration hacking. This operating system comes complete with hundreds of hacking tools for: Information Gathering, Vulnerability Analysis, Exploitation Tools, Wireless Attacks, Forensics Tools, Sniffing & Spoofing, Password Attacks, Hardware Hacking, and Reverse Engineering. Kali Linux was developed by offensive security which is an IT security training company.

Exploitation Tools

Commix
Commix Package Description Commix has a simple environment and it can be used, from web developers, penetration testers or even security researchers to test web applications with the view to find bugs, errors or vulnerabilities related to command injection attacks.

jboss-autopwn

This script is used to gain remote shell access by inserting a JSP shell on the target server. Jboss uses command and upload executions to allow for interactive sessions.

Linux Exploit Suggester

This program is an exploit suggestion script that tracks vulnerabilities and makes suggestions for ways to gain access to administrative rights.

TeethMaltego

This is platform that was developed to provide a map of possible threats to the secure environment. This program can clarify the danger levels of failure points and vulnerable trust relationships within the network.

SET

(Social Engineer Toolkit) is designed for social engineering attacks .This program includes built in custom features which can assist the hacker with designing credible attacks.

ShellNoob

This tool assists with the process of shell development. Prepared scripts are readily available for novice hackers to use.

Crackle

Crackle is a user-friendly brute force password cracking tool. This tool is used during the bluetooth pairing process. It allows the attacker to obtain the short-term key via brute force. With this key and other data gathered can be used to potentially obtain the full network key.

Yersinia

This is a tool designed to exploit weaknesses in network protocols. When running, it appears to be a legitimate operation performing tests on the network, making it difficult to detect by security administrators.

Password Attack Tools

HexorBase

HexorBase is a database application designed to launch brute force attacks against database servers. From a centralized location, the hacker can control, audit, and perform SQL queries on several remote database servers at the same time.

THC-Hydra
THC-Hydra is login-cracking software that supports multiple protocols for attacks. This tool makes it possible for hackers to gain unauthorized remote access to a system.

John the Ripper
John the Ripper combines a variety of cracking modes into one program. This can be custom configured to suit the needs of a particular attack.

Ncrack
Ncrack is a rapid network authentication hacking tool. It was designed to help companies secure their networks by testing all network computers for poor passwords.

RSMangler
RSMangler performs various manipulations a wordlist. This program takes the listed words and generates all permutations and the acronym of the words in addition to other forms of mangling.

WebScarab
WebScarab is designed to be a tool used for exposing the workings of an HTTP(S) based application and identify vulnerabilities.

WiFi Attack Tools

<u>Fern Wifi Cracker</u>
This is a wireless security scanning and attack software program. Fern is able to crack and capture network keys and also runs other network-based attacks on wireless networks.

<u>Wifitap</u>
This tool is used for communications over WiFi networks via traffic injection. Wifitap enables any application to send and receive data packets over a WiFi network using traffic capture and injection.

<u>Wifite</u>
This program can attack multiple encrypted networks in a row. This program can also be easily customized for automation. Hackers can set this program to run without having to watch over it.

<u>Bully</u>
Bully is a new version of the brute force attack. It is similar to other programs that it exploit a well-known design flaw in the WPS specifications.

<u>Aircrack-ng</u>
Aircrack-ng is a WEP and WPA-PSK key-cracking program that recovers keys by

capturing and aggregating data packets. It executes the standard FMS attack, with additional optimizations such as KoreK attacks and the PTW attack.

Sniffing/Spoofing Tools

Wireshark
Wireshark is a penetration-testing tool. This program captures data packets on a network and displays the results in human-readable format. Many resources are available for learning Wireshark, along with a Wireshark certification credential that is widely used by White Hat hackers.

FakeIKEd
FakeIEd (also known as "fiked") is a fake IKE daemon that runs as a background process and attacks commonly-found insecure Cisco-based IPsec authentication setups.

Hamster-sidejack
This program acts as a proxy server that replaces the hacker's session cookies with cookies stolen from another computer. This allows the hacker to hijack the target's sessions. This program works in conjunction with Ferret (also included in Kali Linux), which is a session cookie sniffing program.

Isr-Evilgrade

Evilgrade is a framework that enables a hacker to exploit upgrade vulnerabilities by injecting counterfeit updates. This program comes with pre-scripted binaries, a default setting for fast pentests, its own webserver, and DNS servers.

SSLsplit

SSLsplit is designed for man-in-the-middle attacks against encrypted network connections. Connections are covertly intercepted via an address translation engine and redirected to SSLsplit. This program then terminates SSL/TLS and begins a new SSL/TLS connection to the original destination address. Throughout this process, all transmitted data is logged.

Other Popular Tools

Nmap

Nmap (abbreviation for "Network Mapper"), is used for discovering networks and scanning security. This tool uses raw data packets to find out which computers are available within the network, what software applications are in use, information about the operating systems, and what firewalls are protecting the machine. Kali Linux includes a GUI version of Nmap called 'Zenmap' as an alternative to using the command line.

Metasploit

This program includes a bundle of tools for hacking. IT security admins often use the tools in Metasploit to search the network for holes and weaknesses.

All of these tools are bundled in the open-source penetration testing OS Kali Linux. It is recommended that this OS be installed in a virtual Linux hacking box, which includes the feature of automatically updating repositories.

Chapter 5

Malware: The (Not So) Good, Bad, and Ugly

Malware is an abbreviation for malicious software. There are different classifications of malware, including: Adware, Spyware, Viruses, Worms, and Trojan horses. Once installed on a host computer, malware can be used by a hacker to steal sensitive information, control the computer, and delete or change files. Malware is designed by programmers but used by all levels of hackers for a wide range of purposes. As discussed earlier in this book, reasons may include simple mischief, hurting and organization, stealing information, holding sensitive data for ransom, or more serious crimes.

There are a various ways in which malware can get installed on a computer. One of the most common ways is through email attachments. Sending malware through an email attachments is popular among hackers, because the email application can be used to spread the malware quickly to others. Malware is often attached to software downloads. Users can be enticed to install infected files and programs that introduce the malicious code into their environment. Once these programs are installed, they usually hide from detection software and begin to execute their scripts. Hackers have increasingly begun to implement "drive-by" downloads, this type of attack does not require the user to download or install anything; the malware can install itself on the target computer but simply by visiting an infected website. There are many different types of malware each with its own set of characteristics.

Adware

Adware is designed to make a hacker money. Once the adware is installed on a host machine it displays specific advertisements to the user and can redirect the user's browser to monetized web pages. Adware also has the capability to steal basic user information. This stolen information can be used to target specific ads to the user.

Spyware

Spyware is a more malicious type of adware. Spyware is designed to steal more sensitive information from a user. It can monitor the target's Internet traffic, steal account passwords, and log everything that they have typed into their computers.

Viruses

Viruses are a type of malware that require illegitimate program to host it. Viruses cannot replicate themselves or move two different computers without a working software program hosting it. Viruses can be very harmful to machines.

Examples Viruses:

- Macrovirus (Macro viruses infuse their code into the macros associated with documents, and files.)
- Bootvirus (A boot virus targets and infects a physical component of a computer containing information critical to the functioning of a computer's operating system (OS).
- LogicBombvirus (Logic bombs are small programs that are triggered by an event such as a time, date, the removal of a file, etc.)
- Directoryvirus (A directory virus infects a computer's directory, which contains information about other files and sub-directories throughout the system.)
- Residentvirus (A resident virus stores itself inside a computer's memory, allowing it to infect other files even after the originally-infected program has been deleted.)

Worms

Worms once installed on a host computer behave similarly to viruses however worms do not require a software program to host them. Worms are able to replicate themselves and move between computers through email attachment download link and infected websites.

Examples of Trojan Horses:

- Remote Access Trojans (RATs) (A remote access Trojan (RAT) is a program that contains a back door for remote control of the infected computer.)
- Backdoor Trojans (A backdoor Trojan is a malicious software program that shares the enables a remote hacker to have access to and control an infected computer.)
- IRC Trojans (IRCbots) (An IRC bot connects to Internet Relay Chat as a client, appearing to other IRC users as a legitamate user.)
- Keylogging Trojans (A keylogger Trojan spies on unsuspecting targets. This programs records keystrokes and sends them to the hacker.)

Trojan Horses

Like viruses Trojan horses cannot replicate themselves or move between computers without being attached to a host software program. However Trojan horses can be much more dangerous than either or worms or viruses, because they allow a hacker to remotely control the target machine. Once the hacker is in control, they can steal data, hold critical data ransom, perform illegal activities through the computer, or anything else they choose to do. When used in this way, it is referred to as "Ransomware."

Symptoms of Malware Infection
•CPU usage increases
•Slower computer or web browser speeds
•Difficulty connecting to networks
•Regular freezing and/or crashing
•Modified and/or deleted files
•Appearance of unusual files, programs, or desktop icons
•Installed programs running, turning off, or reconfiguring themselves
•Emails and messages being sent without user input
•Unusual network activity
•Low computer memory
•Programs and files appear or disappear
•File names change

Malware Evasion Tactics
In order to evade detection, malware uses five primary techniques.

Wrapping
During the wrapping process, the malware attaches itself to a normal file. As the appropriate file is downloaded, so is the malware (which usually installs before the regular file). This technique is often distributed

through pirated software and P2P networks. One well-known malware, IceFog is a typically wrapped with the CleanMyMac application and designed to target OS X machines. On Windows, OnionDuke has been wrapped with legitimate Adobe installers distributed over Tor networks by infect computers.

Obfuscation

Obfuscation involves changing binary code it in a way that will not change the way it functions, but completely changes its digital signature. This technique was originally designed to protect legitimate software from reverse-engineering and counterfeiting. Malware engineers adopted the method to bypass antivirus software and weaken manual security. One way to do this is by using XOR encoding. Hiding registry entries, process and file names, URLs, and other useful information can seriously slow down the investigation/reverse engineering of malware.

Packers

These tools are used to compress and encode files, for use in type of obfuscation technique. At runtime, the packer, which is typically infected with the malicious code, will "unpack" the malware into memory to fulfil its objectives. PECompact, UPX, and Armadillo are some common packing tools in use today. Packers are very effective at evading static signature programs.

Anti-debugging

Similar to obfuscation, anti-bugging was created by developers to keep commercial code from being reverse-engineered. Anti-debugging can prevent code from being analyzed in an emulated environments by hackers. The ZeroAccess malware employed a self-debugging function in order to stop external debugging programs. Another example of evasion is malware lying dormant for an extended time period. This allows for bypassing sandboxing solutions, because they only detain code in an emulated setting for a specific amount of time before declaring benign and freeing them into the network.

Targeting

This is when malware is designed to attack systems and/or configurations. The Targeting strategy make sure that the malware is only installed under specific conditions, which enables it to avoid detection in sandboxes because it does not appear that the host is being attacked.

Evasion techniques for malware are constantly evolving. There is a lot of research and development being done in the IT security industry to surpass traditional static signature-based security and move toward behavior-based analysis. The closer that security can be placed to a targeted asset, the higher the chances of being able to identify and defend against it.

Chapter 6
Common Attacks and Viruses

As with any ruthless campaign, a successful hacking attack requires meticulous planning and precise execution. What all successful hackers have in common is their ability to remain undetected, until the time is right to strike. While the methods of attacks greatly vary, they are usually carried out according to these steps.

The Steps of a Successful Hacking Attack

Reconnaissance
Prior to launching an attack, hackers first find a vulnerable target and research the best ways to exploit it. Initially the target could be anyone within the organization. The hacker only needs a single point of entry to begin the process. Phishing emails are common first steps for introducing back-door malware into the secured environment.

Scanning
After the target is selected, the next step is to find a vulnerability that allows the hacker to get access. This is typically accomplished by scanning the network for points of entry. It can

sometimes take months for the hacker to find weak areas in the network.

Access and Escalation

Once a weaknesses is identified, the next step is to gain entry and then escalate. Privileged access is needed in most cases, because it will allow the hacker to move freely within the network. Rainbow Tables and similar tools can help hackers secure credentials, elevate privileges to "admin" or "root," and then gain entry into any system on the network. When the hacker gains administrative privileges, the system is essentially taken over and under the hacker's control.

Exfiltration

With the freedom to move around the network, the hacker can now access the organization's most sensitive data and extract it or worse. Stealing confidential data is not all that the hacker can do; they can modify data or destroy it.

Sustainment

The hacker has now gained unlimited access within the target system. The next is stage is sustainment, wherein the hacker maintains an undetected presence. In order to accomplish this, the hacker may install malware, such as root kits that allow them access whenever they want. With the elevated privileges taken earlier, there is no longer need for a single point of entry.

Assault

This is the stage of an attack when things become malicious. The hacker may change things in the network, or disable the network altogether. During this phase, the hacker is no longer invisible. Because the hacker is so deeply embedded in the network, there is little chance for an effective defense.

Obfuscation

Hackers usually want to hide their tracks, but not all hackers. Some hackers like to leave a signature of sorts in order to take credit for the attack. The intent of trail obfuscation is to confound the forensic examination. Trail obfuscation uses several different tools and techniques, including: backbone hopping, zombied accounts, log cleaners, misinformation, trojan commands, spoofing, and more.

Computer viruses are harmful software programs written designed to enter computers without a user's knowledge or permission. They have the ability to replicate themselves and spread. Some viruses do little more than replicate, while others can cause severe harm to the host program and overall system. These are some common viruses plaguing the Internet today.

1. Memory Resident Viruses

These types of viruses permanently hide in the RAM memory. Once in place, they can take over and interrupt all operations executed by the computer, corrupting programs and files that the user interacts with. They take control of the system's memory and allocates memory space, which they use to execute their own code.

2. Multipartite Viruses

These viruses are distributed through infected files and hide in the memory. Eventually, the virus attacks files on the hard drive by moving to the boot section of the hard drive and later across the entire system.

3. Direct Action Viruses

This virus replicates and takes action when it is executed. When a particular condition is met, the virus goes into action and infects files in the directory, or folder hosting it, and in specific directories in the AUTOEXEC.BAT file PATH. This file is located in the hard disk root directory of and runs operations during the computer's boot process.

4. Overwrite Viruses

This virus deletes the data within in the files that host it. These files are rendered useless once they have been infected. The way to clean a file infected by this type of virus is to delete the entire file, which includes the original data the file contains.

5. Boot Virus

This virus affects the boot sector of the hard disk. This is a critical part of a disk, wherein information is stored together by program that makes it possible to boot the computer.

6. Macro Virus

This viruses infects files that are created using applications and programs that contain macros. These small programs make it possible to automate operations to perform as a singular actions, which saves the user time from having to perform them one by one.

7. Directory Virus

These viruses change the paths that point to the location of a file. By running a program that has been infected by a virus, the user is unknowingly starting the virus program. After infection, it becomes virtually impossible to locate the original file, because the original file and program are moved by the virus.

8. Polymorphic Virus

These viruses use various encryption keys and algorithms every time they infect a different system. Because they are different in each encryption it becomes impossible for anti-viruses to find them with string or signature searches. They are therefor able to create several copies of themselves.

9. File Infectors

These viruses infect programs or executable files. When one of these programs is run, the virus becomes activated, causing the damage it is designed for. The majority of viruses belong to this category and are classified based on the actions that they perform.

10. Encrypted Viruses

This sort of viruses consists of encrypted malicious code and are able to decrypt themselves. These viruses use encryption, which makes it difficult for antivirus software to detect them. Antivirus programs can usually detect these types of viruses when they decrypted themselves and attempt to spread.

11. Companion Viruses

These viruses are file infector viruses, like resident and direct action types. They are called companion viruses, because once they infect the computer they "accompany" other malicious files that infect the machine. In order to perform their infection routines, companion viruses wait inside of the memory until a resident viruses program is run. Direct action viruses can act immediately by making copies of themselves.

12. Network Virus

Network viruses spread throughout a Local Network Area (LAN), and then onto the Internet. Network viruses multiply through shared resources, such as shared drives and folders. When these viruses infect a computer, they search throughout the network to attack new targets. When these viruses finish infecting a machine, they move on to the next, repeating the cycle.

13. Nonresident Viruses

These types of viruses are similar to Resident Viruses by using replication. Nonresident Viruses act as finder modules, which infect more files to every time the module is executed.

14. Stealth Viruses

Stealth Viruses try to fool anti-virus software programs by intercepting their requests to the operating system. They have the ability to hide themselves from many antivirus programs, making them sometimes undetectable.

15. Sparse Infectors

These viruses avoid detection by infecting files only under certain conditions. To minimize the chances of being detected, they might only attack every third time a program is run. They may only infect files with specific sizes, or those whose names begin with certain letters.

16. Spacefiller "Cavity" Viruses

Some program files have an empty space inside of them. Spacefiller viruses attempt to install themselves in these empty spaces, while not damaging the actual programs themselves. These viruses simply attach themselves to the end of files and modify the start sequence of the program, so that it runs the virus first, and then the actual host program. Most of these viruses also implement stealth techniques, so that the user does not see the changes in the file name when the malicious virus is active in the computer's memory.

17. FAT Virus

The file allocation table (FAT) is the segment of the disk used for information connections, which is a critical part of the computer's normal functioning. FAT virus attacks can be particularly dangerous, because they prevent access to sections of the disk where key files are stored. The damage can result in information loss from individual files or entire directories.

18. Worms

Worms are not technically viruses, but programs that behave very similarly to viruses. They have the ability to self-replicate, and can damage a machine. Worms can generally be detected and eliminated by antiviruses.

19. Trojans or Trojan Horses

Like Worms, Trojans are not technically viruses. Unlike viruses, Trojans cannot spread by attaching to other files, and they cannot self-replicate like worms.

20. Logic Bombs

Logic Bombs are not technically viruses, because they cannot replicate. They are not even programs in the traditional sense, but rather disguised segments of other programs. Logic Bombs destroy data on the host computer once specific conditions have been met. These viruses are undetectable until they are launched to run their harmful instructions.

Chapter 7

Hiding Your IP Address

Every time you connect to a network, your computer is assigned IP (Internet Protocol) address. IP address (short for "Internet Protocol address") is the unique number assigned to computer network interfaces. Computers interpret human-readable web addresses as numerical addresses to send data packets to their intended destinations. Emails, web site visits, video conferences, and all other online interactions are coordinated through IP addresses. Your IP address is sent to every server that you visit, those servers keep a log of your visit. This makes it easy for an interested party to track your Internet activity. It goes without saying that when launching hacking attacks, it is essential to conceal one's IP address and remain anonymous. This chapter presents ways in which this can be accomplished.

Why Hide IP Address?

Following are some of the reasons why people want to hide their IP address:

- By hiding the IP address, one can browse anonymously.
- To access websites that are not available to the IP address of a particular Geo location.
- To stay safe from hackers by showing a fake IP to the outside world while keeping real IP concealed.
- Hiding IP means hiding Geo location.
- Hiding IP prevents leaving a digital footprint.

Methods
Proxy Servers

Proxy servers ("Proxies") are servers that you can connect to in order to browse outside of your current network. Once connected to a proxy server, your traffic will be routed through it. This hides your IP, because all of your external connects will use the proxy server's IP. There are different types of proxies offering various levels of anonymity.

Types of Proxy Servers:

- Web-based proxies: These are the most common and easy to use proxies. Users connect you connect to these through web browsers in order to surf the web anonymously.

- Open proxies: These are servers that are left open (due to hacking or user error). Open proxies often insecure and may contain malware. These are generally best to avoid.

- Anonymity networks: These are private anonymous networks that are operated by users donating bandwidth. Anonymity networks are often incredibly slow and not secure.

- Paid proxies: These are software programs that hide a user's IP address to help them mask their internet traffic and physical location while online.

- Virtual Private Network (VPN): These are private networks maintained by businesses or organizations that connect users directly to proxy servers.

- Proxy Chain: These are VPNs that your use TOR (software designed for anonymous web browsing). TOR redirects all Internet traffic using the built-in Linux system package iptables. This is the most reliable method for anonymous browsing and will be discussed further in this chapter.

VPN Software

A VPN works with all internet traffic, including messaging and file transfers. In addition to concealing a user's IP, VPNs are fast, reliable, and encrypt the user's web traffic. VPNs also allow a user to select IPs from different states and countries for access to sites not available in their home location.

Instructions:

1. Download and install VPN software from a trusted website.
2. Manually set VPN settings.
3. Select Internet Options.
4. In the Connections tab, click "Add VPN." This will open the VPN window.
5. Enter in the IP that you are connecting to.
6. Enter a username and password

Many VPN software companies offer a premium subscription. Subscribers get access to thousands of anonymous IPs to choose from.

Using Web-Based Proxies

Web-based proxies are helpful when the user is not on their own computer, because they do not require administrative permission to download software. There are several websites that provide proxies for use. Proxy.org is a trusted site that maintains an updated list of available proxies.

Instructions:
1. Choose a proxy site.
2. Select the URL box.
3. Enter a website address to visit.
4. As long as you continue to browse through the proxy, your IP address will never be visible to the websites you visit.

Using a web-based proxy will make browsing noticeably slower, because the traffic is first rerouted through the proxy, then reinterpreted before it is sent to your machine.

As an alternative, you can configure your browser to use a proxy server. Both Google Chrome and Mozilla Firefox can be configured to automatically hide IP addresses through proxy servers. This requires the download and installation of a plug-in for the web browser.

How to Verify that the IP Has Changed

To verify that the IP has changed, type "my IP address" into your browser before and after using a proxy service, and compare both IPs to make sure they are different.

TOR Browsing
Tor is free software for anonymous online browsing. Tor directs online traffic through an international network consisting of thousands of relays. Tor is designed to protect the identity

of users, and conceal their communications by confounding Internet monitors.

Tor encrypts Internet data, including the IP address, numerous times and sends it through a several randomly-selected Tor relays. Every relay decrypts a single layer of encryption, revealing only the next relay on the path. The final relay decrypts the last encrypted layer and sends the original data packets to the destination without sharing, or even knowing, the original IP address. This method eliminates any single point in the network at which the identities of the two communicators can be determined by Internet monitors.

How to Connect to the TOR Network:

1. Download Tor Browser (https://www.torproject.org/projects/torbrowser.html.en)

2. Click the download link that matches your Operating System, and save the package on your computer or USB storage device.

3. Click "Save File," and start downloading Tor Browser:

Install Tor Browser
You do not have to install the Tor Browser as you would most software; you can extract it to a USB storage device and run it from there.

1. Navigate to the folder in where you saved the Tor Browser package.

2. Right-click on the Tor Browser file and click "Open."

3. Select the language you would like to use and click "OK."

4. Select the location where you would like to install the Tor Browser.

5. Once you have selected your location, click "Install."

6. Click "Finish" to complete installation.

Selecting "Run Tor Browser," you will proceed to launch the browser.

Your first time you starting the TOR Browser Bundle you will be asked how you would like to access the Internet. Choose "Direct Access" if your access to the Internet is not restricted. If your Internet access is censored or restricted the select the "Bridge Configuration." This configuration is detailed, and you will have to follow the instructions carefully. The settings can be changed in the TOR browser bundle at any time from within the TOR browser bundle without having to reinstall the software. Once you have configured and launched the Tor Browser, you can connect to the Tor network without additional configuration.

Chapter 8
How to Hack an Email Password

Hacking an email account can provide access to a large amount of useful information about the target and everyone on the target's contact list. This chapter discusses ways to hack an email account.

1. Keylogging:

Keylogging is one of the most effective and widely-used ways to hack all sorts of information. Though some networks are so secure that even the most experience hackers would have difficulty finding vulnerabilities, most can be cracked with a keylogger. Keyloggers are a type of software (and also hardware) that run in the background of a target computer, and it record every keystroke that is entered, including passwords, then sends the logs to a server that the hacker can access by logging into an online account that comes with the keylogger program.

Although many experienced hackers use complex methods for remotely installing keyloggers (e.g. injecting programs into file downloads) any level hacker can install a keylogger program, as long as they have access to the target computer. Physical keyloggers are very easy to install; they are physical devices that look similar to a USB drive and can covertly be slipped into the back of a desktop machine. Once installed, they run in complete stealth mode and are undetectable to user and most security software. The highest-quality keyloggers support "remote installation" making it possible to install on target computers regardless of the physical distance.

2. Phishing

Phishing is a popular method used to steal email passwords. Phishing is a method wherein a hacker uses Phish (fake webpages or applications) to steal sensitive information from a target.
Phishing is a play on "fishing," based on its similar strategy to catching fish with a trap. Technically Phishing is a technique to steal a target's password using the phish or counterfeit pages. The hacker sends fake webpage links to the target, and when the user logs into the counterfeit page with their credentials, a log file is generated containing the username and password. Successfully executing a phishing attack requires some knowledge of web page design and scripting language.
Malware-based phishing uses malware to spread phishing messages. For instance, an

infected email account automatically sends messages to everyone on the victim's contact list. These messages typically include links prompting the receivers to install the malicious program onto their computers or devices.

In some cases, phishing malware is included in gaming apps for user's mobile devices. One popular gaming app contained malicious code that allowed the developers to steal email IDs and passwords of the users. In these cases, the app actually works, and the victim may is unaware of installed malware that has infected their device.

Method 3: Social Engineering

Social engineering an effective alternative for hackers to steal users' login credentials. This involves impersonating someone in order to trick the target into voluntarily providing their login credentials.

One way to do this is to create a false account containing an address that appears to belong to a friend or colleague of the target. The hacker then deceives the victim, saying (for example) that they need their login information to sign them up for something. Hackers often impersonate administrators or customer service personnel to gain trust from their victims. Spam emails might claim that the target's Google account was hacked, and they need their username and password to verify if the account is compromised.

Method 4: Stealing Cookies

There are a number of ways for hackers to steal cookies from other users' sessions and to insert them into their own web browser. Tools such as Wireshark Cookie Injector and GreasMonkey allow hackers to sniff out cookies on a local network and use them to take over the victim's session. This is most easily done on public Wi-Fi networks. Some hackers prefer "war driving" to find and exploit open wireless networks. Oncea cookie has been stolen, the hacker can login to the victim's account and read their emails, send messages, and change the account settings to block the actual owner.

Although new hacking software is developed every day, the underlying strategies for hacking email accounts tend to remain the same. The wholesale integration of email, social media, and phone numbers has opened territory for new and innovative approaches to the above strategies.

Chapter 9

Spoofing Techniques

Spoofing attacks are when hackers use tools to impersonate devices or users on a network. The purpose for spoofing is to launch attacks against network targets, spread malware, steal data, or evade access controls. There are several types of spoofing attacks that hackers can use to accomplish this. Some common methods include: IP spoofing, email spoofing, ARP spoofing, URL spoofing, website spoofing, MAC spoofing, GPS spoofing, and DNS server spoofing. This chapter discusses common spoofing techniques.

IP Spoofing

IP address spoofing is a frequently-used spoofing method. When launching an IP address spoofing attack, the hacker sends IP packets from a misleading (or "spoofed") IP address in order to disguise its source. Denial-of-service (DOS) attacks often utilize IP spoofing to flood networks and devices with packets that seem to come from legitimate IP addresses.

There are two ways in which IP spoofing attacks are used to overload target systems. One method is to flood the selected target with packets from several different spoofed IPs. This is done by directly sending the target more data than it can handle, causing it to fail. The other technique is to spoof the victim's IP address and send packets to several different targets on the network. When another computer receives the packet, it will automatically return a packet in response. Because the spoofed packets look like they were sent from the target's address, every response will be sent to the target's IP address, quickly flooding it.

With distributed denial-of-service attacks (DDoS), the hackers is attempting to consume bandwidth and drain resources by flooding the target with a multitude of packets in a short period of time. In order to conduct the attack, the hacker spoofs many source IP addresses, making it extremely difficult for security to track and stop the attack.

IP spoofing attacks are also used to bypass IP address-based authentication. The process can be difficult (requiring modification of thousands of packets at once), and is typically used when trust relationships exist between machines on a network. Trust relationships utilize IP addresses (instead of user logins) to verify computers' identities when they are attempting to access systems. This allows malicious parties to employ spoofing attacks, impersonating computers that have access permissions, and to bypass network security measures.

ARP Spoofing

ARP (Address Resolution Protocol) is a protocol used for resolving MAC (Media Access Control) addresses to IP addresses for the transmission of data. With an ARP spoofing attack, the hacker sends spoofed ARP messages through a local area network (LAN) in order to link the hacker's MAC address with the IP of a legitimate computer on the network. This type of attack results in data, intended for the target's IP address getting directed to the hacker instead. Hackers often use ARP spoofing to steal information, transform data in-transit, or shut down traffic on a LAN. ARP spoofing can only work on LANs that use Address Resolution Protocol.

DNS Server Spoofing

The Domain Name System (DNS) associates domain names with IP addresses. Machines connecting to the internet or another private network rely on DNS to resolve URLs, email addresses and domain names into their equivalent IP addresses. Networks use a DNS server, which is provided by an Internet service provider (ISP) or the user's organization. With DNS server spoofing, the hacker injects data into the Domain Name System (DNS) resolver's cache. This causes the server to return a fraudulent IP address so as to reroute a specific domain name to another IP address. The hacker is then able to redirect all traffic, to a server of their choice, where they can manipulate or steal data that passes across. The new IP address, in many cases, will be point to a server that is controlled by the hacker and contains a variety of malware. These attacks are often utilized to spread worms and viruses.

MAC Spoofing

This is a technique for changing the Media Access Control (MAC) address of the network interface on a device. This address, which is factory-coded on the network interface controller (NIC), is supposed to be unalterable. However, many drivers enable the MAC address to be changed. There are tools which can force an operating system to believe that an NIC has whatever MAC address the hacker chooses. The process of disguising a MAC address is called "MAC spoofing." This involves changing a machine's identity, and can be done relatively easily.

When a user spoofs their own MAC address to protect their privacy on a network, it is referred to as "Identity Masking." A user may choose to do this if the Wi-Fi network connection is not encrypted. A hacker, in order to elude being tracked, can choose to spoof their computer's MAC address. This way they can move around the network's permissions while hiding their identity. Some secure networks utilize MAC filtering to prevent unauthorized access. Hackers use MAC spoofing to gain access to networks and do launch attacks. By MAC spoofing, hackers can place the blame for any illegal activity onto a network user.

Website Spoofing

Website spoofing involves creating a counterfeit website, with the intention of deceiving targets into providing sensitive data, such as passwords, banking information, or any other type of useful data. Typically, the spoof website will recreate the design of the spoof website and have a similar URL. A highly sophisticated attack could involve the hacker creating a "shadow copy" of the Internet by redirecting all of the target's traffic through the attacker's server.

There are other types of spoofing, including GPS spoofing. However these are the most common forms of spoofing in use today.

Chapter 10

Mobile Hacking

In the hacking world, mobile apps present a plethora of opportunities. In contrast to controlled network environments, mobile devices connect to the Internet on public Wifi networks. The unprotected binary code running in mobile devices can be accessed, inspected, altered and exploited by hackers. Binary code is what machines read to run applications; it is what is download when a user acquires mobile apps from an online app stores. Advanced hackers exploit of binary-based susceptibilities to compromise apps on mobile devices. The advanced hacker does this by conducting covert code modifications or injecting malicious code into an app's binaries. Code alterations and code injection attacks are launched in two ways:

The hacker modifies the binary to change its behavior. For instance, disabling security controls, evading business rules, overriding licensing restrictions, paying for ad displays in a mobile app (possibly marketing their malicious script it as a security patch, crack, or include it within a new application.

The hacker can inject malicious code into the binary of an existing mobile app, and then repackage the original app and publishing it as a new app, to be distributed on app stores. Fortunately today hacking mobile devices does not require hackers to conduct such advanced operations. Android smartphones, in particular, can execute penetration and security tests from hacking Android apps. With the help of a few mobile hacking tools, a novice hacker can launch powerful attacks on mobile devices. This chapter discusses hacking tools that are effective for mobile hacking.

The Android Network Hacking Toolkit

This toolkit is designed for penetration testing for network vulnerabilities with the use of a mobile phone. The toolkit contains a variety of apps that help hackers find vulnerabilities to exploit.

Nmap for Android

Nmap (short for network mapper) is a powerful network scanning (port finding) tool. Nmap works on Unix OS, Android, and Windows mobile OS. Once the scan is complete, the results are emailed to the hacker.

AnDOSid is a DOS (denial of service) attack Tool for Android. This is very powerful tool, because it can use DOS to shuts down a mobile device, or DDOS to overload a web server, all from a mobile phone.

SSHDroid- Android Secure Shell
SSH (short for "Secure Shell") allows a hacker to connect to a device from a PC and execute administrative commands.

AndroRat
AndroRat (short for "Android Remote Administration Tool") is a remote administration tool that is used to control another device without requiring physical access. A hacker can manipulate other devices with this app.

DroidSheep
DroidSheep is used for extracting important information from a target's social media accounts. This app hijacks the sessions of social media activities conducted on a network.

Kill WIFI
Kill WIFI is enables a hacker to cut off anyone's WiFi access to a network. This app's clear and interactive interface make this app easy to use.

SpoofApp
SpoofApp enables a hacker to disguise a phone number when making a phone call. This app can also change the hacker's voice and record a

phone conversation. This app requires SpoofCards to use.

WhatsApp Sniffer
This tools is designed to hack a target's private WhatsApp files by using their Wifi hotspot. This works in conjunction with the WhatsApp application.

APK Inspector
APK Inspector is designed to reverse engineer Android applications. This allows the hacker to obtain the source code of any android application and edit it to remove license and credits. Some hackers use this to analyze Android apps to learn the coding behind it.

Eviloperator
This software automatically connects two targets in a phone call making them think that they called each other. The hacker can then record the conversation.

Burp Suite
Burp Suite is a platform for performing security testing of web applications. Hackers can utilize this as a testing lab for planning real attacks.

dSploit
This is a bundle of tools used to conduct network security assessments on mobile

devices. It allows for such covert attacks as password sniffing and traffic manipulation.

<u>FaceNiff</u>
This is an Android app that enables a hacker to sniff and capture online session profiles over a shared WiFi network. FaceNiff uncovers passwords for Twitter, Facebook, Blogger, Amazon, Tumblr, and various other online accounts.

Sample Cell Phone Hacks

There are many different ways to hack into a passcode-locked cell phone and gain access to the personal data inside. Today virtually everyone carries a smart phone and uses it to store all sorts of private information, including: contacts, financial information, texts, emails, photos, etc. Here we examine ways to hack into two different phones via bypassing the secured lock screens. Both hacks exploit security bugs and neither require software tools; however, both strategies require physical access to the phones.

<u>Crash the Lock Screen (Android 5.0)</u>
If Android device uses the standard password lock screen, follow these steps to bypass it.
Tap the "Emergency Call" option on the lock screen, and use the dialer to enter ten asterisks

(*). Then, double-tap to highlight the asterisks and select "Copy." Paste back it into the same field in order to double the number of characters. You then repeat the process of copying and pasting to until the field stops highlighting the asterisks.

Return to the lock screen, and tap on the camera shortcut. Next pull down the notification shade and tap on the "Settings." You will then be prompted to enter a password. Hold down the input field and choose "Paste." You then keep pasting into the password field until the lock screen crashes. You will then have full access to the phone.

Trick Siri (IOS 9)

Tap the Home button to call up Siri. Ask her to open an app that you do not have. Siri will report that you do not have that app and offer to help you find it in the App Store, while displaying to you the App Store icon. Tap on that icon, and the phone will open a restricted browser window. At that point, select "update" and open the last app, or you can tap two times on the Home button for the task slide to appear. You then swipe over to the active front screen task. At that point, you have circumvented the passcode iPhone (5 and 6) lock screen.

These two examples exploit flaws in the mobile OS security features of these two phones.

There are other ways to hack through mobile security software, most of which require hacking tools and a degree of skill. The mindset of a hacker is that everything can be exploited; it's simply a matter of determination.

Chapter 11

Penetration Testing

Penetration Tests examine weaknesses in a network by attempting to find and exploit them. These weaknesses can be found in software at these specific points of entry:

- Backdoors in Operating Systems;
- Design flaws in the of the software code;
- Inadequate software security management implementation;
- Utilizing the software application ways it was not designed to be used.

Pen Testing can be successfully accomplished through either manual or automatic processes. It is generally targeted toward these endpoints:

- Wireless networks;
- Servers;
- Network endpoints;
- Network security devices (Firewalls, Routers, Intrusion Programs, etc.);
- Wireless and Mobile devices;
- Any other exposed areas, such as vulnerable software applications.

Actual Pen Tests do not stop at this level. The main goal is to get as deep as possible inside of the IT infrastructure and get access to the assets of the target. The goal is both to just strike hard the first time and continue to strike undetected for as long as possible.

White Box, Black Box, and Gray Box Testing

There are three kinds of Pen Testing that can be used to find vulnerabilities in web applications: White Box Testing, Black Box Testing, and Gray Box Testing.

Black Box Testing

In an actual cyber-attack, the hacker does not know all of the specifications of the target's IT infrastructure. Consequently, the hacker will launch a thorough, brute-force attack in the hopes of finding a vulnerability to exploit.

With this type of Pen Test, the hacker has little or no information about the particular Web Application, its source code, or its architecture. Therefore, this type of test can be very time consuming. When possible, the hacker will use automated processes to uncover the system's weaknesses.

White Box Testing

With White Box Testing, (also known as "Clear Box Testing") the hacker has complete knowledge of and access to the Web Application's source code and software architecture. Due to this, a White Box Test can be completed much more quickly than a Black Box Test. Another advantage is that a more thorough Pen Test can be accomplished.

This approach also has disadvantages. Because the hacker has full knowledge of the software, it could take longer to decide where to focus on system and component testing and examination. Also, when conducting this kind of test, more advanced tools are usually required such as, code analyzers and debuggers.

Gray Box Testing

This type of test is an amalgamation of the Black Box and the White Box Tests. The hacker has limited knowledge of the internal workings of the target software. This is usually limited to just gaining access to the application code and architecture diagrams.

With Gray Box Testing, the hacker uses both manual and automated testing processes. Using this approach, the hacker can focus time on the areas of the software that they are most familiar with and try to exploit any vulnerabilities. Employing this method increases the likelihood that of finding "security holes" as well.

Penetration Testing Teams

The idea of one-person Pen Testing is not always practical. Sometimes the best types of Pen Testing is done with multiple testers working as a team. There are three types of Pen Testing Teams: The Red Team, The Blue Team, and The Purple Team.

The Red Team

The Red Team is comprised of members who perform the actual Pen Testing. Their main goal is to emulate the mindset of a hacker who is attempting to penetrate all of the weaknesses and vulnerabilities in the system. The Red Team attacks all possible angles.

The Blue Team

The Blue Team consists of personnel within the infrastructure itself (typically members of the IT Security team). Their main goal is to protect and defend against all attacks from the Red Team. The Blue Team must be proactive and vigilant in order to successfully defend the system against attacks.

Both the Red Team and the Blue Team can be considered two opposite sides of a coin. The goal of these two teams is to strengthen the security of the IT infrastructure by sharing feedback with each other. This, however, does not always occur. In such cases, there is need for a Purple Team.

The Purple Team

The Purple Team can be viewed as the composite of both the Red Team and the Blue Teams. The Purple Team takes the security strategies of the Blue Team and also the weaknesses and vulnerabilities exposed by the Red Team. The Purple Team then combines this information into a singular description which can be shared by all of the teams in order to implement a comprehensive policy of continuous security improvements for the organization.

The Purple Team can be considered as a "bridge" between the Red and Blue Teams. This team helps to facilitate continuous integration between the attackers and defenders. The Purple Team should be a neutral and separate entity in order to avoid bias.

Types of Penetration Tests

In this section, we will discuss various types of security penetration tests, including: Network Services, Web Applications, Client Side, Wireless, and Social Engineering.

Network Services

This is the most commonly-used pen test. This involves finding security vulnerabilities and network infrastructure. This test can be conducted from within the network or remotely. If it is possible, it would be best to attack from both positions. This type of test involves probing the following:

Firewall configuration testing;
Firewall bypass testing;
Stateful analysis testing;
IPS evasion;
DNS attacks which include:
- Zone transfer testing;
- Any types or kinds of switching or routing issues;
- Any other required network testing.

Some common software packages that are examined in this test:

Secure Shell (SSH);
SQL Server;
MySQL;
File Transfer Protocol;
Simple Mail Transfer Protocol (SMTP);
Microsoft Outlook login pages.

Network Service testing is not a particularly deep type of testing. That level of testing takes place in the Web Application Test.

Web Application

This type of test is more extensive than the network Pen Test. With Web Application Testing, security vulnerabilities and weaknesses are exposed in Web-based applications. Components such as Silverlight, ActiveX, Java Applets, and APIs are all inspected. Much time is needed to properly and thoroughly test Web applications.

Client Side

This kind of test is designed to reveal security vulnerabilities in software that can be easily exploited on a target client computer. This includes Web browsers (e.g. IE, Chrome, Firefox, and Safari), content creation software packages.

Wireless

This test involves probing all of the wireless devices on the network (tablets, notebooks, smartphones, etc.). The following are also tested for security vulnerabilities:

- Wireless protocols;
- Wireless access points;
- Administrative credentials.

In many cases, the Wireless test is performed at the target site, because the Pen Testing tool has to be in relatively close proximity to the wireless network.

Social Engineering

This type of test consist of attempting to get sensitive or proprietary information by tricking someone within the organization to reveal such things. There are two types of Social Engineering tests:

- Remote testing: This includes deceiving a target into revealing sensitive information through electronic means. This is often accomplished by creating and launching a Phishing E-mail attack.

- Physical testing: This involves use of physical methods or presence to gather sensitive
data. This can include dumpster diving, impersonation, threats, physical theft, deceptive messages, etc.

Computer Network Exploitation (CNE) Vs Computer Network Attack (CNA)

There are two main threats that a hacker can present to a target organization:

- Computer Network Exploitation (CNE);
- Computer Network Attacks (CNA).

Computer Network Exploitation (CNE)

With this kind of threat, a network can be utilized to target a victim computer network for the purposes of extracting and gaining confidential information, sensitive data, and classified documents. The computers, devices, and servers within the victim network are compromised by any means possible. This type of attack does not usually happen in the corporate sector, but rather with government (particularly military) agencies around the world. CNE is viewed as "spying" by many.

Computer Network Attack (CNA)

With this type of attack, the objective is to destroy at information residing on the computers throughout the target network. A CNA uses a data stream to conduct an attack against the target network and completely incapacitate it. CNA is considered "sabotage".

This chapter provided an overview of Pen Testing, including techniques involved, Pen Testers; and descriptions of common Cyber-attacks. There are many other methods an advanced hacker can utilize, but only a comprehensive Pen Test can reveal all of the unexpected vulnerabilities and weakness in an IT infrastructure.

Chapter 12

Digital Footprints

Today online privacy is increasingly harder to achieve. Internet Service Providers (ISPs), advertisers, and governments are becoming more adept monitoring your online activities. Fortunately, tools are available to help you remain anonymous. This chapter discusses ways to avoid leaving digital footprints that can used to track and identify you. Some strategies are more complex than others. However, these tools can help you to mask your identity and cover your tracks on the Internet.

TOR (The Onion Router)

The Onion Router (Tor) uses an extensive network of computers to direct your Web traffic through several encrypted layers to conceal the origin of the traffic. By downloading and installing the Tor Browser Bundle, you will have everything necessary to use browse anonymously. Although the TOR network is especially designed for online privacy, government agencies have occasionally found ways to identify individuals and groups inside of the network. Consider TOR to be one part of a comprehensive strategy for concealing your identity online.

VPN

VPN solutions such as TorGuard and Private Internet Access. These services basically allow you to mask your traffic. Your real IP address is hidden from the outside world, and your online movements are indecipherable to ISPs and governments. TorGuard also offers its "stealth" VPN service for free. This solution makes government detection much more difficult to accomplish.

DNS Leak Testing

Although you may be using a privacy service, such as a VPN, to conceal your IP address, you could still possibly be leaving clues to your identity through your DNS traffic. You can detect if you are leaking your DNS information by going to DNSLeakTest.com, and running their extended test.

If the results display your third-party DNS service (like TorGuard), then you are good. If id displays your ISP's DNS information, then you have a DNS leak. By following the steps on the how to fix a DNS leaks web page, you will be able to solve this problem. Test yourself again to ensure that your privacy is secure.

Virtual Machines

Your browser isn't the only entry point for others to identify you and track your activity.

PDFs and other apparently benign files can serve as homing beacons that alert entities when you access planted files. To prevent such compromises of your privacy, open suspicious files inside of a virtual machine.

To do this, open a Linux distribution inside of VirtualBox, configure it according to your preferences, and save a snapshot of your VM. Then, download the suspicious file, and shut down your virtual machine's connection to the Internet. Next, open the file; view the file, and then shut down the VM. The next time that you want to view a file inside of your VM, you will have your snapshot already prepared.

Blocking Third Party Cookies

Third-party cookies are among the most common ways that advertisers follow your browsing behaviors. If you visit two websites that use the same advertising service, you can assume that the advertiser is logging that information. All major browsers have the ability to disable tracking cookies. Prying eyes have a much more difficult time following the pages you visit without the use of third-party cookies.

Blocking Geolocation Data

Many sites use location data to offer particular services, and provide targeted ads. Mapping applications have obvious reasons for logging location data, however the same technique can be utilized to help identify you. Most browsers allow users to toggle location data. It is recommended that turn it off and keep it off. If you are on the Internet without using a proxy or VPN, you are giving out your IP to every server that your data passes through. That information can be used to track you.

Do Not Track

Browsers can send an optional "Do not track" HTTP message to Web servers. You can enable this in the browser's settings. For this to work however, a Web server must be configured to respect this message. There is no requirement that websites obey this setting, so this does not guarantee protection from trackers.

Plug-in Management

Even when your browser is configured to hide your identity, plug-ins can still be utilized to compromise your anonymity. To minimize this risk, avoid running plug-ins completely. This, however, will render many popular websites unusable. Using a hybrid approach can help to solve this problem.
You will need to configure your browser to ask your approval before running any plug-ins. Next, make sure that you are running plug-ins.

JavaScript Blocking

JavaScript has the possibility of leaking out identifying information. It can also give out detailed information about your setup to Web servers, including: plug-ins you have enabled and the screen size are you using. Small bits of information like that can add up to make following your usage profile easier for observers. Unpatched JavaScript breaches can be exploited to fool your browser into giving up even more detailed information.

In order to be actually anonymous, you will have to disable JavaScript. Doing this, however, significantly limits your Web browser. Many sites use JavaScript for their core functionality. By installing browser extensions such as NoScript or scriptno, you can control which domains are allowed to run JavaScript in your browser.

Ghostery Browser Extension

This browser extension enables you to block a variety trackers from the web, and it displays which tracking services are being used on websites that you visit. It also allows you to enable and disable tracking on the fly.

Privacy Badger Browser Extension

The Privacy Badger add-on monitors when sites try to track your online movements, automatically protects you from future tracking attempts, and automatically improves its blocking list the more you browse.

HTTPS Everywhere Browser Extension
SSL a good way to keep your Web traffic protected from prying eyes. To avert packet sniffers your Web traffic should always be sent through SSL connections. Not every website supports SSL, and even those that do sometimes default to unencrypted connections anyway. The HTTPS Everywhere extension forces SSL connections on websites.

Disable WebRTC
Your browser can give away much of your network data to any web server that requests it. If WebRTC is enabled on your browser, your internal IP can be discovered by any website, and even your real IP while using a VPN. For Firefox, go into about:config, and turn media.peerconnection.enabled to "false." You can also utilize this add-on as a toggle. Chrome, however, does not allow you to turn off WebRTC completely.

BetterPrivacy Browser Extension
Even when you are blocking cookies, some websites can still track you using Local Shared Objects (LSOs) also referred to as "Flash cookies." these won't be a problem for you as long as you have Flash disabled. You can

configure Flash to block LSOs, however that would disrupt some Flash content. The BetterPrivacy plugin (for Firefox) allows you to tightly manage LSOs the same as you do with normal cookies.

Browser Leaks Testing
If you want to confirm that your privacy settings are working, go to BrowserLeaks.com, and examine all of the data that your browser is revealing. This toolset is not exhaustive, but still very effective in most cases.

Use different email addresses for each site that when you sign up for a user account.
You can create countless free email accounts, and configure email forwarding to direct all of your messages to a single inbox. This also has the benefit of being able to identify the sites sell your information to third-parties and spammers.

Even the most cautious hackers can be vulnerable to attacks against their anonymity. Some strategies to protect privacy online can be time consuming and inconvenient. It is, however, imperative for budding hackers to master the art of stealth on the Internet.

Chapter 13
Tips for Ethical Hacking

Ethical hackers conduct the same attacks against IT systems and individuals that malicious hackers do. An ethical hacker's purpose, however, is to uncover any system weaknesses for the benefit of an organization. This chapter contains tips aspiring ethical hackers.

Ethical Hacking Considerations

<u>Work Ethically</u>
This means working with high morals and principles. Everything that you do as an ethical hacker must support the organization's goals and have no hidden agendas. This also includes reporting all findings. Do not misuse any information. Trustworthiness is the bottom line.
<u>Respecting Privacy</u>
All of the information that you obtain during testing must be kept confidential. Do not read confidential information about the organization or the employees.
<u>Involve the Organization</u>
Allowing the organization to oversee your activities can help you gain trust and support throughout your ethical projects.

Avoid Crashing Systems

Poor planning can cause a hacker to unintentionally crash the system that they are trying to help protect. This is often due to misunderstanding the strength of the tools and techniques that they are using. Running too many tests at the same time can cause systems to lock up, corrupt data, trigger system reboots, account lockouts, etc. Websites and applications are particularly susceptible to crashing. Vulnerability scanners can help to control the number of tests that run on a system at the same time.

Hacking Tips

Understand How Operating Systems Work.

Not all operating systems function the same way. In order hack successfully, you will have to do much research. An OS can affect the methodology, feasibility, and impact of a hacking plan. It is very important to know your way around OS directories and their commands. Covering your tracks and file editing are important techniques in hacking. If you do not know where specific system files and logs are located, you run the risk of getting caught. By taking the time to learn the directory layouts and commands of all of the operating systems, you will save a lot of time and energy after you get into a system.

Know a Little Bit about Everything.

As a hacker, it is important to have an expansive skill set that goes beyond basic script kiddy exploits. Being proficient in coding and scripting, knowing languages like Ruby, Python, Perl, and C, along with having other general IT skills, such as network security and analysis will benefit you in all aspects of ethical hacking. Being able to identify what is happening within the network and designing your own custom exploits and scanners can make the difference between you getting caught and being able to freely gather all of the information you need.

Have a Full Understanding of the Network.

When planning an attack on a network, it is beneficial to have as much information about it as possible beforehand. Find out how it is set up and decide on an attack vector. Then plan out what you will to do for each vector. Doing this will help you to keep all of your steps organized, so that you remember everything that you have already done and all that you have left to do. This will also help prevent you from going back and repeating the same steps repeatedly, and spending time trying to remember where you were in the attack. Repeating tasks can create a lot of unnecessary and noticeable traffic on the network, possibly exposing your attack.

Know Your Hacking Tools.

Having an in-depth understanding of the tools you are working with, what they do, and how they work will greatly assist you with getting them function properly. Not knowing how to use your tools can cause serious damage to the system. Tools can be unpredictable and quirky. It is important to make certain that the tools you are using are designed to what you are attempting to do.

Know Alternative Approaches.

When you attack a system in a different and unexpected ways, it makes it much more difficult for security systems to catch you. If you can construct unique ways to exploit systems and networks it will make your attack hard to detect and even harder to stop. Always consider a variety of ways to attack the target system. Unique attack vectors are make it hard for security to identify the origin of the attack, because primary-level investigations look for traditional tactics.

Document Everything.

Clients usually want a breakdown of everything you did, so that they can reproduce the attack in future tests. Using notes and screenshots are easy ways to keep track of your exploits. Also, be sure to save everything, including: output, logs, the arguments passed to your tools, and all of the traffic to and from your target. This can also help to verify all of your hard work.

Know How to Communicate with Members of the Organization.

You can be a wonderful hacker in terms of your technical ability; however, if you cannot effectively communicate with clients, peers, and project managers, your work loses value to them. Even if you have accomplished something that will save their entire IT system, this means little to a high level manager who cannot comprehend the language that you are using.

Get Involved with the Hacking Community.

Although keeping up with every new development in the IT security industry is impossible, you must still make time to participate in some key hacking groups that share information and important content that you can use with your own projects. This will help you get to know other hackers, keep up with what is going on in the industry, and learn about new tools. These are all important things that will help you to stay competitive in your field.

Know How to Exploit Bugs When You Find Them.

When you discover a bug, it is important to show why the vulnerability is an important, and to demonstrate the associated risks by exploiting it. Any hacker can simply identify a bug, but a good hacker will take the time to effectively exploit it.

Do Your Own Research.

Do not simply rely on other developers' and hackers' tools and research. There are never enough tools to tackle every situation, so it is important for you to be able to create your own. If y discover something interesting or new, research it and share the results with the rest of the hacking community.

By applying these tips to your practices as an ethical hacker, you will build the foundation for a long and rewarding career in the world of IT security.

Chapter 14

A Few Tips for Computer Safety

Keeping your computer healthy is essential for security. Before concerning yourself with strong passwords, encrypted communications, and private browsing, you must protect your computer against hackers and malware. Likewise, it would not make much sense to hide your valuables inside of a building and then leave the door wide open.

This chapter discusses how to properly maintain your software and use tools to protect your computer against malware infections and malicious hacking attacks. Although the security tools discussed in this chapter are for Windows OS, (the operating system most vulnerable to such threats), Apple OS X and GNU/Linux systems are also at risk, and users should still implement these strategies and tools.

Anti-virus Software

Avast is an excellent free anti-virus program for Windows. This program is easy to use and regularly updated by anti-virus experts. Users are required to register once every 14 months, however updates, registration, and the program itself are all free.

There are many other popular commercial anti-virus programs other than Avast, such as Clam Win. This alternative to Avast lacks some important features needed in a primary anti-virus program, however, Clam Win has the benefit that it can be run from an external drive; so, it can be used to scan devices that are not allowed to install software on.

Tips for Effectively Using Anti-virus Software

- Avoid running two anti-virus programs simultaneously. This might slow your computer down or cause it to crash. Always uninstall one antivirus program before installing another.

- Make certain that your anti-virus program allows updates. Some commercial tools that come already installed on new computers must be paid for and registered and or they will not receive updates. All of the software recommended in this chapter supports free updating.

- Make sure that your anti-virus software updates itself routinely. New viruses are designed and distributed daily, and your computer will become vulnerable if you fail to maintain new virus definitions. Avast automatically searches for updates when you are connected online.

- Enable your anti-virus software's virus-detection feature to always be on. Different tools have different ways for doing this, but most offer such a feature. It may be called 'Resident Protection,' 'Realtime Protection,' or something similar.

- Regularly scan all of files on your computer. This is not necessary every day, particularly if your anti-virus software is always on. However, you should do this regularly. How often may depend on such circumstances as how recently you have connected to unknown networks, whom you have shared USB drives, if you regularly receive suspicious attachments by email, or if someone on your network recently had a virus.

Preventing Virus Infections

You must be cautious when you open email attachments and files received online or downloaded from the Internet. Avoid opening files that you receive from unknown sources. If you must do so, first save the attachment on your machine, then open the appropriate application (e.g. MS Word or Adobe Acrobat). By using the program's file menu to manually open the attachment (instead of double-clicking on the file or letting your email program automatically open it) you are far less likely to get a virus.

Before putting removable media (i.e. CDs, DVDs and USB sticks), into your computer consider the potential risks. First make sure that your anti-virus program updated and its scanner is running. Disable your OS's AutoPlay program, which may be used by viruses to attack your computer. By switching to open source software, you can help to prevent many virus infections, because it is usually more secure and less often targeted by virus writers.

Preventing Spyware Infections

When browsing websites watch out for browser windows that appear automatically. To help prevent webpages from fooling you into downloading malware on your computer, close pop-up windows by closing the dialogue box (clicking the "X" in the upper right corner), instead of clicking "Cancel." Blocking pop-us and selecting "no-script" options in your browser can also help improve security by preventing the browser from automatically running malicious programs that are sometimes contained within webpages.

Firewalls

A firewall is the computer's first program to see data coming in from the Internet. This is also the last program to deal with outgoing data. Similar to a security guard, a firewall receives, analyzes, and makes judgements about incoming and outgoing data. A good firewall will allow you to select access permissions for every program on your computer. When a program attempts to connect to the outside world, a firewall will block the attempt and warning you, unless it is familiar with the program and verifies that it has permission to make a connection. This is to prevent malware from spreading or welcoming hackers to your computer. A firewall provides two lines of defense and an early-warning system to alert you of security threats.

Keeping Your Software Up-to-Date

Software programs are often complex, making it likely that some of the software contains errors, and some of these errors may weaken your computer's security. Software developers work to uncover these bugs and create updates to fix them. It is critical that you frequently update your computer software, including the OS.

Other Tips

- Only install essential programs on the computer, and be sure get to them from reputable sources.
- Uninstall software that you no longer use.
- Always disconnect from the Internet when you are not your computer, and completely shut it down overnight.
- Do not share your passwords. Disable automated services that you are no longer using.
- Consider switching from commercial operating systems and software to open-source software.

These security measures will help to make your computer safer, but not completely safe. The best way to ensure online security is to keep all of your software updated and read current literature on hacking and everything else related IT security.

Conclusion

Ethical hackers among one the most important contributors to our rapidly-evolving digital society. Virtually all human activity is tied to technology in one form or another. Countless, anonymous hackers possess the tools and capabilities to cause harm to governments, businesses, and individuals. The financial prospects alone make criminal hacking very attractive. It is the mark of a great person to forgo such temptations and utilize their skills to help make the Interne safe for others. Ethical hackers, in the popular vernacular, are paid professionals simply doing a job. What all White Hat hackers know, however, is that there is more to ethical hacking that money; there is a respect for the privacy of individuals, a need for a healthy Information Superhighway, and there is a place for ethical principles in every walk of life, including technology.

To become a full-time professional ethical hacker, you must learn the inner workings of computers and networks. You must know software development from an inside perspective. You must also be able to get inside of the minds of Black Hats and understand their drives and motivations. This is all necessary to successfully protect the digital infrastructure. This chapter include some information on how you can begin your journey down the road of IT security.

A career in ethical hacking requires analytical problem solving and good communication skills. Hacking also involves a balance of technical skills, intelligence, common sense, and good judgement. Ethical hackers are in charge for analyzing servers and systems to identify any security risks. They conduct penetration tests to uncover security vulnerabilities in a system by using existing hacking tools in addition to custom tools that they make themselves. Other responsibilities ethical hackers have include:

- Giving suggestions on how to mitigate weaknesses;
- Advising developers concerning security needs;
- Revising security policies and procedures;
- Training IT staff as other personnel

Requirements for IT Security Jobs

Entry-level ethical hacking jobs generally require a Bachelor's Degree in Computer Science. Security certifications can also be very helpful in proving requisite knowledge.

Major Certifications for Ethical Hackers:

- CEH: The Most Basic and Widely Recognized Certification
- Penetration Tester (GPEN)
- Certified Ethical Hacker (CEH)
- GIAC (Global Information Assurance Certification)
- Offensive Security Certified Professional (OSCP)

For aspiring ethical hackers, the CEH certification may be the best way to go, since it is the broadest. This certification is provided by the EC-Council and designed to provide IT security professionals with a solid understanding of security threats, risks assessments, and proactive countermeasures through traditional lectures and labs.

This book provided you with an introduction to the world of hacking. You now have enough information to access the necessary tools, build your virtual hacking box, and begin learning the art and science of hacking.

Thank you again for downloading this book!

Finally, if you enjoyed this book, then I'd like to ask you for a favor, would you be kind enough to leave a review for this book on Amazon? It'd be greatly appreciated!

Click here to leave a review for this book on Amazon!